The Strange Case of R.L. Stevenson

RICHARD WOODHEAD

The Strange Case of
R.L. Stevenson

RICHARD WOODHEAD

Luath Press Limited

EDINBURGH

www.luath.co.uk

First Published 2001

The paper used in this book is recyclable. It is made from low chlorine pulps produced in a low energy, low emission manner from renewable forests.

Printed and bound by
Cromwell Press., Trowbridge

Typeset in 10.5 point Sabon by
S. Fairgrieve, Edinburgh 0131 658 1763

for Gill

Contents

Introduction

I WAS SEVEN YEARS OLD when I first became aware of the name Robert Louis Stevenson. I can easily recall the bright autumn day. I had been visiting a school-friend (in the Headingley district of Leeds) and his mother was taking me to the bus-stop on my way home. She was a brisk, bespectacled, intelligent woman with a cheerful laugh and a keen interest in encouraging children to read books. 'Richard,' she said, 'your first two initials are R.L. – that means you have something in common with Robert Louis Stevenson. You would like his books. Start with *Kidnapped*, not *Treasure Island*.'

I persuaded my parents to buy me a copy of *Kidnapped*, and I read it, I think within a few days. I was captivated by the adventure of David Balfour setting off on his journey. I was terrified by the dangers of the house of Shaws. I was carried away by the shipwreck, the flight in the heather, the whole story. Of course, I went on to read *Treasure Island* and *The Strange Case of Dr. Jekyll and Mr. Hyde*. Later, I progressed to the more 'difficult' *Master of Ballantrae* and, much later, to *Weir of Hermiston*, with its complex psychology. I read some of Stevenson's essays and travel writing. I never gave up reading Stevenson, even when my undergraduate friends in the early 1960s derided him as 'unfashionable'.

During my career as a hospital physician, I would read some fiction (as much as time allowed) at the end of each day, probably as an antidote to the relentless reality of sickness. I would also read biography. Stevenson's life story, dominated by travel and illness, culminating in his early death in a far-off land, was particularly fascinating. It seemed to be generally assumed that his lung disease was tuberculosis or, to use the old term, consumption. This was the reason for his journeys to France, Switzerland, America and the South Seas; this was something crucial to his life and work. And yet any physician reading, for example, Graham Balfour's official biography, with its guarded but revealing references to symptoms and treatment, might question the label of tuberculosis that has so often been attached to the name of Stevenson.

After retiring from my hospital post early in 1997, I had the time to pursue personal interests more seriously. I read everything that I could find relating to Stevenson's life, guided for much of the way by Booth and Mehew's highly authoritative, eight-volume, *The Letters of Robert Louis Stevenson*, with its precise identification of the time-scale of events and accurate pointers to sources of information. I came to realise that it would be impossible to prove or disprove a diagnosis of tuberculosis, and that a factual account of Stevenson's illness would be unsatisfactory and inconclusive. By that stage, I knew that the exact diagnosis was less important than the way the illness was perceived by Stevenson, by his family, and by the many doctors who treated him. As a physician myself, I was particularly interested in the personality, attitudes and prejudices of the doctors. I had to look at this within the context of the 19th century, but there were many parallels with the modern world.

I have told the story in the words of five doctors who treated Stevenson at different periods of his adult life. This is not a biography or a work of scholarship. It is a work of fiction, with the 'narratives' apparently written towards the end of the 19th century (not all at the same time). The doctors existed in real life, but only a limited amount of factual information about them is available (and very little indeed concerning their private conversations with Stevenson). Therefore I have invented some of their views and most of the dialogue, but I believe that much of this could be true. Using the wealth of available information concerning the life of Stevenson, I have planted the fictional elements of the story within a matrix of facts in such a way that everything described could have occurred within the known framework of time and place. As far as possible, I have derived Stevenson's views (and some of his words) from his own written work. Information on sources is given at the end of the book.

The story of Stevenson's illness offers more questions than answers. Was Stevenson master or victim of his illness? How did this affect his writing? Did Fanny (his wife) use the illness to further her own ambitions? How far were the doctors influenced by their own histories and prejudices? My hope is that readers will enjoy reaching their own conclusions.

Part One:
Dr. Andrew Clark's Narrative

Chapter One

TUESDAY THE TWENTY-EIGHTH of October 1873 was my forty-seventh birthday. I mention this as a matter of fact, as a pointer to the precise date, and not to suggest that the anniversary would interfere in any way with the routine of my daily work. I took breakfast at speed, no more than a quarter of an hour from start to finish, and at the same time scanned my letters from the morning post. There wasn't enough time (there never has been) for me to follow my own dictum 'thirty-two bites for every mouthful of food': I am not a gentleman of leisure. And so across the corridor to my study to prepare for the day's first consultation, which would, as always, start promptly at 8 o'clock. I cannot deny that I am one of London's most fashionable physicians; as such, I have to maintain self-discipline and a capacity for long hours of work in order to see all the patients who want to consult me here at 16 Cavendish Square. Don't misunderstand me. I don't look upon this as self-sacrifice. I admit that I revel in the demand for my services. I feel relaxed only within the walls of my consulting room. I maintain that work is a remedy, not an affliction. Sometimes I summarise my advice with the words 'labour is health: lead a full life, active and occupied', but in general I confine this robust approach to patients whose illnesses are more imagined than real.

My study is also my consulting room. A room lined from floor to ceiling with books: row upon row of leather-bound volumes, some pristine with bright gold embossed titles on their spines, some – old friends – frayed and faded. My weakness for buying new books, and my continuing astonishment that I can afford to do so, ensures that the sharp smell of fresh leather always pervades the room, overwhelming any hint of fustiness; it is a library of new wealth, not a museum. There are books on medicine, of course, and books on philosophy. There are adventure stories and works of fiction. There are theology books, carefully arranged by subject and size to cover the wall facing my chair. And at the top of this wall, painted in ornate white lettering on a polished oak board, the words 'Glory to God' are displayed. I do not believe in hiding the depth of one's religious belief. My standing in the High Church community, doubtless bolstered by the patronage of Cardinal Manning, has done no harm to my consulting practice.

I have a mirror hung on the wall, just inside the door of the study. This is primarily for the use of patients, but I confess that I look at my reflection several times a day: a reflection framed in gilt, like a portrait. Thus I remind myself who I am. The distinctly grey hair and beard are outward manifestations of a middle age which is in every way more agreeable than the struggles of my earlier years. The black cravat, the white wing collar, the morning coat, the dark grey trousers: a uniform worn throughout the working day which, in my case, tends to correspond to the sum of my waking hours. This is the mirror image of a successful doctor, but it is also the image of a man who needs reassurance, a man who sometimes half expects to see the frightened face of the orphaned 13-year-old medical apprentice. I thank God that He has given me the power to work and to improve my station in life. You can be sure that I will continue to use this power for as long as it is granted to me.

It was my birthday, but I had no reason to expect that it

would be memorable, the morning spent at home, as usual, in my study, which serves as my consulting room. Many of the patients eager to dispense guineas in my direction are *malades imaginaires*, suffering from hypochondriacal afflictions which I am particularly good at recognising (often within a matter of minutes) and, unlike so many of my professional colleagues, sympathetic in handling. I have taught myself the art of never seeming to hurry my patients and I am never censorious. Such cases are the basis of my thriving private practice, but I also have considerable experience in treating serious illness.

On that particular day, I reached the hour of 12 noon (my customary time for taking a light lunch in the study) with an unusual sense of irritation. Even for me, a succession of patients wishing to discuss the details of their indigestion did not make an interesting morning's work, and I was aware that I would need to spend several hours that evening in writing up personalised diets for each patient. This still remains my usual practice, although I know that I have been criticised from time to time for making my detailed dietary instructions too generalised. Needless to say, I have heard the much repeated 'joke' that my patients at any fashionable London dinner party can be identified simply by observing who does not take soup. I continue to insist that soup, any soup, is bad for the digestive process.

My butler, Reynolds, served out lunch of two boiled potatoes and a small mutton chop as I washed my hands. A careful washing of the hands, a time to pause for thought, a ritual performed after (but not before) the examination of each patient.

'I'll need the carriage ready to get me to the hospital by three o'clock,' I told him. 'How many more patients are waiting to see me?'

'There are no further patients with appointments, sir, but there is a young man who has come in off the street hoping to consult you. I've explained that you may not be available to see him.' Corpulent, and somewhat stately in manner, Reynolds exuded that concerned, protective air which for many years I have found so comforting. In reality, however, many of the patients who come to consult me arrive without an appointment, and at that stage of my career I never turned anyone away. In any case, a young man 'off the street' was unlikely to represent another case of indigestion, and there was at least the possibility of something more challenging to whatever diagnostic skills I might possess. Admittedly, the fee offered was likely to be modest, but this would balance the excessive sum that had been pressed on me earlier in the day by a dyspeptic lady, well known in society.

'And have we seen this young man before?' I asked, as I picked at the mutton chop, my abdominal muscles already tense with the feeling that I should be pressing on with my work.

'No, sir. He comes from Edinburgh, and at present he's staying in Bayswater with friends.' After a pause he added, with the corner of his mouth turned down, 'I understand that he is a law student. His name is Stevenson.'

This is how I first heard the name of Stevenson. This is why I remember my 47th birthday.

As soon as I had finished my lunch, and was seated again at my desk, Reynolds ushered in the young man. Loping through the doorway, Stevenson swiftly stole a glance at himself in the mirror before he approached me. I indicated a chair whilst at the same time fixing him with a steady, and I hope a friendly, gaze. He was a decidedly thin young man, with a curiously narrow chest which was not disguised by a somewhat tattered black velvet jacket with threads hanging down where there should have been buttons. His shirt was black as well and he wore a necktie that appeared to have been cut out of an old curtain.

'I'm very pleased to meet you, Mr. Stevenson.' I probably exaggerated my Aberdonian accent, or at least I didn't restrain it, in recognition of my patient's Scottish origin. 'How long will you be staying in London?'

'That rather depends on you, Dr. Clark. I'm expected to take the preliminary examination for one of the Inns of Court, but I don't know if my health is up to it. I've been in London for just three days, and I feel unwell, decidedly unwell. I've always been subject to coughs and fever, but the sore throat and pleurisy of the last few days have dragged me down worse than ever. How can a man be expected to study the law when he hasn't got the strength to pick up a textbook?' He added that he had already spent two years in Edinburgh on legal studies, and found the charms of learning conveyancing and copying documents to be somewhat limited.

'Let's start from the beginning.' I flipped back the silver lid of the ink-well and then slowly, deliberately, dipped in the nib of my pen, scarcely disturbing the quiet, smooth surface of the blue liquid. 'What is your full name? What is your age?'

'My age is nearly 23, and my full name is Robert Louis Stevenson. Louis spelt L-o-u-i-s, with the s pronounced, and not L-e-w-i-s, a spelling I abandoned four or five years ago for reasons that won't interest you. Please make sure that you spell Stevenson with a v and not ph: I am the grandson of Robert Stevenson, builder of some twenty lighthouses, including the Bell Rock itself.'

I looked at him with a new respect. The first sight of the

scrawny, ill-dressed student had been misleading; my usually faultless gauging of social status had, for once, failed.

'With such a family background, Mr. Stevenson, I'm surprised that you're not an engineer yourself.'

'Well, I did enrol as a student of engineering at Edinburgh University when I was 16. It seemed to be in the natural course of events: my father assumed that I would graduate, and then join the family firm. I learnt many things during my years at the University, but not much of this was concerned with engineering, and my dear father eventually agreed that I should abandon the subject. Truancy was my specialty – a highly developed skill, you might say – but at least I did have a paper accepted at the Royal Scottish Society of Arts.' He leant forwards with his elbows on my desk and smiled at me. 'On a New Form of Intermittent Light for Lighthouses', by R.L. Stevenson. I don't imagine you've read this magnum opus, Dr. Clark?'

I averted my eyes, preferring to ignore his teasing question. The truth is that I found it difficult to suppress my distaste for this young man's flippant dismissal of educational opportunities. Understandable distaste, perhaps, in the light of my own background. I was orphaned at the age of seven, and then placed in the hands of foster parents. I served a long apprenticeship to a doctor in Dundee before I was accepted for classes at the Edinburgh School of Anatomy, but I couldn't afford to enter the University itself. It was fully ten years after I had started in medical practice before I was awarded a University degree as such. Yes, ten years of unremitting work before the University of Aberdeen graciously awarded me the degree of Doctor of Medicine. And by that stage I was already an Assistant Physician at The London Hospital! If only I had been given Stevenson's opportunities as a young man, I would have grasped them and used them to the full. This dilettante student was a walking insult to the innumerable young Scotsmen who yearned for the chance to advance themselves by hard work.

'Let's return to your medical history.' I adopted an air of studied calm. 'You mentioned that you've always been subject to coughs and fever.'

'For as long as I can remember, doctor, I've had a particular talent for illness. I was a sickly child: my schooling was interrupted time and again by fevers. I managed little more than a year at Edinburgh Academy, and finished up at a small school for delicate and backward boys. As a result of this, I never learnt Latin properly, and my English spelling is atrocious. You can blame my chest for that. My mother tells me that I had croup when I was two years old and, from then on, I was the victim of recurrent, hacking coughs and fever. I've spent more days in bed than you can imagine, and more nights in feverish terror than I care to recall. I couldn't have survived without the devoted care of my nurse. She was a kind of angel to me, an angel of the night who calmed my febrile imaginings. I've never been free of the threat of fever, Dr. Clark, and it's difficult to explain to you the feeling of disappointment, despair even, which comes over me every time it starts again. I always hope that it will be the last time, but I hope in vain.'

By this stage, he was out of his chair, a strange, attenuated, gesticulating figure, pacing up and down the room. His flow of speech was interrupted when he looked up at the wall, and read the words 'Glory to God' on the oak board, at which he sat down again, this time with his head sunk between his hands, his light brown hair flopping in front of his eyes. 'Does this make sense to you, Dr. Clark?' came the worried, weary question.

His words did make sense, and the way that he spoke them evoked in me a chilling reminder of my own years of illness.

'Yes, of course it does, Mr. Stevenson. Your account is eloquent. Now tell me what's happened in the last few days; I need to know why you've chosen today to come and see me.'

'That's easy to explain,' he replied. 'I developed a sore throat when I was staying with my cousin Bob in Portobello last week. As usual, it's developed into fever and a touch of pleurisy. Have I made everything worse by travelling to London? My friends Professor Colvin and Mrs. Sitwell insisted that I should come and see you. They've installed me in Bayswater, and will no doubt look after me, but what about the future?'

As he was speaking, I listened to his words and I looked at his face: I looked into his face. Why were his eyes so compelling? Brown, almost black, nothing unusual about the colour, but shining, definitely shining. A moist, friendly, vulnerable quality. Over-active lacrimal glands perhaps? And there was something else, something which I have never seen on another face. His eyes were set unusually far apart so that he seemed to encompass me, almost engulf me, with his gaze. A gaze not threatening, not unblinking, but demanding involvement and engagement. Yet it was not in any way an uncomfortable experience.

'Have you had any other symptoms? Have you lost weight? Have you had any blood spitting?'

'No, no, no. My weight is nothing to speak of, but it never has been. As for blood-spitting, it's not a hobby of mine, I'm glad to say.'

I always take a detailed history from my paying patients. This establishes a relationship and demonstrates my interest in their well-being; while they are talking I closely observe their physical characteristics and mannerisms. After further questions and answers relating to meal times and diet, I began my physical examination. Laënnec introduced the stethoscope into medical practice barely twenty years before I started my apprenticeship in Dundee and I like to think that few other doctors have made better use of the Frenchman's invention than I have: anyone who accuses me of being old-fashioned should take note of that.

The appearance of the young Scotsman, minus his shirt, was impressively frail. His chest was perhaps the narrowest that I have ever seen in a man of this age, and his arms were long and spidery with tapered, nicotine-stained fingers. He turned the scales at eight stones six pounds, a light weight indeed for a man five feet ten inches in height. I was relieved to see that his shoulder blades did not stand out like wings, an appearance so often seen in consumption, but of course this possible diagnosis was at the front of my mind. Consumption or tuberculosis: by whatever name the disease is known, it remains the plague, the 'white plague' of this century, and of many bygone centuries.

My knowledge of the many insidious and ugly ways in which consumption can present itself is based not only on my medical studies but also on direct experience. Some eight years before the day I examined Louis Stevenson, I myself had contracted consumption, and it was then that I learnt something of despair and resignation. I also learnt about hope, and then I learnt about belief, belief in my cure by milk diet. Four years later, I had to relearn all these lessons when the disease recurred, interrupting what others have described as the meteoric rise of my medical career, just at the time that I was moving my residence and consulting rooms from Bloomsbury to the more elegant surroundings of Cavendish Square.

Although my profession has taught me to bear the sufferings of others with equanimity, I found myself praying that there would be no signs of consumption as I continued my examination of Louis's chest. My small white hands with their rather stubby fingers ('surprisingly gentle', I have heard said) worked their way along their habitual routine: a routine which has become so familiar and so practised that sometimes my hands appear to be separate from me, to have an existence of their own. I laid the middle finger of my left hand against the front of his chest, and then tapped against it with the tip of my right index finger, leaning towards him and listening carefully to the sound of the percussion note, the note which results from the vibration of air in the lung, and which indicates the consistency of the lung tissue itself; I then repeated the procedure up and down the front and the back of the chest. Louis, obviously well-versed in the ways of doctors, sat calmly as I then examined his chest with the stethoscope (a modern two ear piece instrument, beautifully fashioned from nickel, ivory and vulcanite), through which I listened to the breath sounds: the coarse transmitted noise of inhalation, followed by the gently fading expiration, like the sound of a sleeping baby. And the signs were uniform, with every part of his lungs sounding as good as any other part.

After I had completed my examination, intimate, yet distant, and I hope reassuring in its method, I returned to my desk and wrote some notes while Louis re-dressed.

'I'm glad to say that I find no sign of disease, Mr. Stevenson.' Needless to say, it was not necessary for me to name the disease of which I found no sign, nor would I ever have considered doing so under such circumstances.

'Thank you, doctor,' replied Louis, 'but I wonder what I should do to get well again.'

'Perhaps a return home is all that is needed to settle the symptoms. A comfortable house, loving parents and familiar surroundings can be remarkably good for health. I can state categorically that you are not fit to sit an examination for the Inns of Court, and I will supply a written opinion to that effect.'

Louis smiled, his apparently mocking expression belied by the pleading, shaky tone of his voice. 'When my mother was ill with chest trouble ten years ago, we spent three months in Nice and Menton. The climate of the French Riviera was most beneficial. Would you advise such a trip for my illness?'

I paused before replying. 'Well, there is a London physician, or gynaecologist to be precise, called Bennet, who advocates the beneficial effects of the Riviera for sufferers from lung disease. I believe that he still lives in Menton during the winter months. However, as I say, I find no actual signs of lung disease in yourself.'

'That may be, doctor, but much as I love my parents, I can't face another winter in Edinburgh. The east wind is my bitter enemy.'

'Have you discussed the matter with your parents? Would you want your mother to accompany you, to look after you?'

He was on his feet again, pacing to and fro in front of me.

'When I set off for London, I told my mother that I was going to Carlisle. A trip to the south of France would be impossible without financial help from my parents, but I would need to be alone.'

I turned towards the window and looked out over

Cavendish Square, a green island in a turbulent sea of horse-drawn traffic. I tugged at my watch chain and glanced at the hour.

'Perhaps you should now explain to me the real problem, Mr. Stevenson.'

Chapter Two

IT WAS WELL INTO the afternoon when I left the house, too late to be certain of reaching Whitechapel in time to start the ward round promptly at three o'clock. During my early years as a physician, I had a reputation at The London Hospital for punctuality, but the demands of private practice have made this increasingly difficult to sustain; I confess that, these days, it is not unusual for 60 or 70 medical students to wait half an hour or more for me to arrive.

As I have done so often, before and since then, I glanced back as my carriage, pulled by a pair of overweight bay cobs, drew away from 16 Cavendish Square. I have never achieved total belief in the demonstrable fact that this is my house. This handsome five storey building, with its majestic chimney-stack, its colonnaded front porch and its sturdy black railings: this is my house. Not a bad achievement for an orphan from Aberdeen!

I can claim that my property and status are the result of unremitting work, and I can say that my determination to drive myself hard is as strong as it has ever been. Daily contact with sickness and poverty at the hospital simply reinforces this motive power for professional advancement; if this results in self-enrichment, then it also acts as insurance for my family against the penury which blighted my own childhood. I make no apology for this, and I say again that work has been my salvation. When my first wife died at the age of 31, it was the demands of my job that protected me from the ravages of grief and allowed me to make a natural progression, five years later, to a second marriage, now the basis of domestic harmony at Cavendish Square. I see myself as the rock on which Helen and the children can depend for their anchorage, and I will do whatever is necessary to fulfil this role. Fortunately, I belong to a profession that offers rich rewards for utilising my natural sympathy with human suffering. At times, I can scarcely believe my good fortune, and I freely acknowledge the debt that I owe to famous patients who are willing and eager to recommend my services to their friends and relatives. Had it not been for the cholera epidemic of 1866, Mrs. Gladstone would not have visited The London Hospital. And if she had not visited the hospital and heard a patient sing my praises, then I would not have become physician to the Prime Minister. It is Mr. Gladstone's patronage – based, I think I can say, on mutual respect and understanding – which has done more than anything else to enhance my reputation as a trustworthy and sensible physician. It is no secret that Mr. Gladstone continues to seek my opinion, sometimes on a day to day basis, and there have been a number of occasions when he has curtailed his activities specifically on my advice. In this way, the orphan from Aberdeen has influenced the course of history.

I admit that, as my carriage rattled through the gates of The London on my 47th birthday, I felt a sensation which the place has often evoked in me: a glow of pride, surely allowable to the Senior Physician of this great voluntary hospital. My election to the post of Assistant Physician some twenty years earlier had astonished the supporters of my better connected rival, Dr. Ramskill. Indeed, I had heard myself referred to as a 'poor Scotch beggar', an invalid thought to have no more than a few months to live. Ramskill was himself elected to the hospital staff, as my junior colleague, at a later date; since then, he has had a number of years in which to reconsider his attitude towards me. My behaviour towards him has always been courteous: studiously courteous.

I stepped out of my carriage at the front door, casting aside the theology book that I had been reading, in a rather desultory fashion, during the journey to the hospital.

'I must apologise for my late arrival.' It was an apology which neither required nor received a reply from the House Physician, who was waiting for me on the steps leading up to the entrance. 'Have we many patients to see today?'

'Perhaps we should concentrate on just one of the wards, sir,' came the answer. 'The hospital's full to overflowing, and the other wards aren't prepared for the number of students attending your round.'

In those days, The London was invariably 'full to overflowing'. The large number of acute cases – patients requiring immediate admission – caused continuous pressure on the availability of beds in the hospital. This had the effect of transferring control of the admitting system from the Governors of the hospital to the resident doctors, who were always available to make rapid decisions on such matters. The only option left to the Governors at times of crisis was to close the hospital to all admissions other than accidents and emergencies, and this was a course of action that they took again and again. To their credit, though, they also took the longer view that fund-raising was required for much needed expansion of the buildings. For my part, I hated to see extra beds and other signs of overcrowding on the wards, and I never raised any objection when I suspected the nursing staff of hiding some patients from sight during my visits.

About twenty medical students joined me at the start of the teaching round. As usual, we were escorted by the ward's head nurse, freshly turned out with white apron, white cap and close-fitting linen cuffs. The floorboards, scrubbed clean and yet with the stains of years ingrained; the beds neatly spaced and yet too close together; the fire lit and yet the air too cool. The familiar fusty atmosphere, with its hint of feculence, assaulting the nostrils for those first few sniffs, and then fading, blunted, unnoticed, into the background. Sometimes, this smell would take my mind back, transiently, to the 1866 cholera epidemic, when over two thousand patients in the district of The London had died by the first week of August, and the hospital had been crammed with victims, half of whom hadn't survived; it was during this sombre period that I had been promoted to the status of 'full physician' at the hospital, an accelerated promotion born out of the vagaries of disease.

Surrounded by medical students, I consciously adopted the theatrical pose that was expected of me. The main interest of my boyhood years was dramatic poetry and playing centre stage has never been a burden to me: it is a role that suits my personality. 'Now, gentlemen, I perceive that our first patient is better.'

'How can you say that without examining the patient?' The question came from a bright, clean-shaven student, a regular attender who doubtless knew the answer but was willing to play the game.

'Yesterday,' I replied, 'her hair was untidy and her clothing was askew. Today her hair is combed and her clothing is neat. She is better, and no further enquiry is needed.'

It is more than likely that the students were unconvinced by this example of deductive reasoning, and indeed the woman's appearance might have owed something to the attention of the nursing staff, but the patient herself was both delighted and encouraged by my words. In this way, I hope that I demonstrated something to the young gentlemen.

'Observation, observation, observation.' It is my belief that repeating a word three times can multiply its power without obscuring its meaning.

As we moved from patient to patient, I relaxed into teaching by anecdote and epigram, my words cutting into the church-like silence of the ward. As always on these occasions, I recalled past diagnostic triumphs, embellishing the stories with dramatic gestures. And I recalled past mistakes as well, mistakes which could instruct the ignorant and the arrogant, but not my real mistakes, the ones that I had expunged from my memory. I have no doubt that the students can recall my tales long after they have forgotten the details of their pathology lectures. Colleagues who mock my alleged verbosity and tendency to overgeneralize should take note of this.

'Gentlemen, diseases are the outcome of constant and apparently unimportant violations of the laws of health. No detail is too trivial for the physician's attention. Make sure that you have a record of everything that the patient tells you: it is from such information that the diagnosis will emerge.'

'Is it possible, Dr. Clark, to take a detailed history from every patient who comes into the hospital, at a time when the number of emergencies is increasing day by day?'

'It is certainly possible, simply by working at it. Thomas Carlyle, addressing the students of Edinburgh University a few years ago, declared that 'work is the grand cure of all the maladies and miseries that ever beset mankind'. Perhaps we can't necessarily apply this dictum to our patients, but we can certainly apply it to ourselves. Remember that work never kills; worry does. You are privileged to be students of medicine, which is the metropolis of the kingdom of knowledge. You must work at all aspects of your medical studies and avoid over-specialisation, which tends to narrow the mind.'

'And would narrow the income at Cavendish Square, no doubt.' The muttered comment from somewhere amongst the students was just audible. I chose to ignore it.

Conscious as I was that my utterances were becoming increasingly Delphic, I was relieved when the flow of words came to a natural halt as we approached the patient in the far corner of the ward. She was perhaps twenty years old, pale and emaciated, with her cheek-bones sharply visible under the thin skin, and her face clammy with sweat. Her breathing was rapid and laboured as she gasped for the air that could never be sufficient for her needs. Scarcely conscious and too weak to move, she turned her eyes towards me with an expression of undeniable hopelessness. Immediately, instinctively, I was drawn to her. I felt like a doctor. I held her hand as the bed was curtained off from the rest of the ward. Gently, and as though all the time in the world was at my disposal, I listened to her chest with my stethoscope, carefully moving it from point to point and placing it with exquisite precision, like an instrument of healing. I held her hand again and then looked into her eyes, just for a moment. Speech was not necessary: I felt that, in some indefinable way, I had eased her suffering.

I led the way from the dying girl's bed to the other end of the ward. Speaking in a low voice, but unable to suppress the dramatic tone that was second nature to me, I asked the students to make a diagnosis.

'It looks like consumption.' The answer came from the same fresh faced, eager young man who had questioned me earlier on. Why is it that, in any group of students, there is always one who seeks attention and dominance? My experience suggests that, irritating though it may be to the other fellows, such a student is likely to progress to a successful career in the medical profession.

'You say that only because consumption is a common disease,' I replied, 'but whether you call it consumption or tuberculosis of the lung, you can't make a positive diagnosis unless you demonstrate signs of a cavity within the lung itself: hence my careful use of the stethoscope. If you can't demonstrate that there is a cavity, then there is no other method of diagnosing the disease with any degree of confidence, and therefore there is no means of proving or disproving your opinion until such time as a post mortem examination is held. In the case of this unfortunate girl, the stethoscope reveals clear signs of cavities: the breath sounds at the apex of each lung are distinctly 'amphoric', like the whistling, echoing noise produced by someone blowing across the neck of a jam jar. It is a noise with a peculiar cavernous, ominous quality. She is suffering from galloping consumption.'

'What is the treatment, Dr. Clark?' It was him again.

'Over two hundred years ago, John Bunyan described consumption as 'the captain of all these men of death', and this is still the case today. My namesake, Sir James Clark, no relation of mine, said: 'we might as reasonably expect to restore vision when the organisation of the eye is destroyed as to cure a patient whose lungs are extensively damaged by tuberculous disease.' In other words, there is no useful treatment for advanced disease, except to ease the patient's suffering with opium. Having said that, spontaneous healing of more localised tuberculosis is a commonplace event.'

I take pleasure in quoting the aphorisms of Sir James Clark. It was he who advised me of the value of a milk diet when I was suffering from the disease myself. There may be no proven effective treatment for consumption, but I hold to the belief that the milk diet saved my life. However much this statement may be derided as illogical by those whose minds are limited by the horizons of science, I know it to be true.

It was early evening, dark and wet, by the time that I had finished the ward round and was on my way back to Cavendish Square. Rain pattered on the roof of the carriage and splashed up off the pavements, faintly illuminated by the greenish-white gas light of the street lamps. Progress towards the West End was slow, hampered by the density of omnibuses and Hackney carriages, which intermittently brought the traffic to a standstill. The snorting of the horses and the clatter of their hooves, the raucous shouting of the drivers, some friendly, some aggressive: all sound was dampened by the steady rain. Cocooned in my carriage, I felt as weary as an actor coming off stage; I knew that, as usual, I would be occupied in writing letters and instructions until past midnight. I squeezed a finger inside my wing collar which, whatever its size, always seemed to be too tight. There were times, fortunately few in number and brief in duration, when I felt an almost overpowering urge to break free from my chains and escape. But I knew that my strength would revive after I had reached home and allowed myself an hour for dinner with Helen. Just an hour: that would be enough. My wife has always happily accepted my limited availability for meals and other domestic matters.

I didn't attempt to read my theology book on the way home. My mind was occupied with the case of Louis Stevenson, the young man who had initially irritated me with his flippant approach to educational opportunities, but had then captivated me with an emotional description of literary ambition. Louis clearly felt that his father had dismissed literature as a mere pastime, unfairly insisting that his son, having abandoned engineering, must become a lawyer. The only child of loving and much-loved parents had acquiesced, out of respect for his father as well as to gain the financial support that would result from his obedience. The division of minds, however, could not be disguised for long, and a serious rift had developed between Louis and his father after a quarrel over religion had taken place.

Louis's father had discovered a document detailing the 'constitution' of the 'L.J.R.', initials standing for 'Liberty, Justice and Reverence', a so-called club endorsing atheism and rejecting all parental teaching. This 'constitution', formulated by his cousin Bob, had been the source of some amusement to Louis, but at the same time it did reflect his burgeoning agnosticism, which he had then confessed to his father. The barely controlled rage of his father's response had gradually given way to deepening gloom and a daily volley of accusation and antagonism. Louis had challenged the Calvinistic beliefs of the family and had wounded their pride in him; Mr. Stevenson had let it be known that he was praying daily for his son's salvation.

Louis had told me something of his own tormented, guilt-ridden reaction to the pain that he was causing his parents, but it was pain that had to be inflicted and endured if he was to escape from the comfortable, stifling atmosphere of parental love and control. It was not surprising that, after months of conflict, his delicate health had broken down: he had lost the will to combat illness.

As I understood it, Louis had fled to London, not with any real intention of entering the Inns of Court, but for solace and advice from his friends Sidney Colvin and Mrs. Sitwell, whom he had first met during a visit to Suffolk earlier that year. Mrs. Sitwell, who had connections in Menton, wanted him to escape there, to recover from family conflict and to develop his literary talent.

Within a few minutes of annoying me with his facetiousness, Louis had engaged my sympathy. He was weak and vulnerable but at the same time he had shown an interest in me as a person and not simply as a functionary. My Scottish roots may have helped our mutual understanding, although, in my experience, roots are more likely to divide than unite Scots. For whatever reason, I felt that I could identify with his sense of artistic ambition, despite the fact that, when I was aged 22 myself, I had been earning my living as a Royal Navy surgeon at Haslar with no option of abandoning my profession for vague literary pursuits.

At first sight of Louis's emaciated frame, I had suspected and feared consumption. By the time I had finished examining him I had realised that his history of recurrent cough and fever more likely indicated a different condition: a mundane disease with the unattractive name of bronchiectasis, which actually was first described by Laënnec. A five syllable word is often difficult to understand; usually, it is even more difficult to explain, but I must attempt to do so. When part of the lung tissue becomes

infected it sometimes shrinks, pulling on the walls of the adja-
cent bronchi (the medium-sized airways, or tubes, in the lungs),
which become widened and distorted. In this way quite a simple
lung infection during childhood can result in permanent damage
to bronchi, which become misshapen, like hollow spindles or
sacks. These damaged tubes are then themselves vulnerable to
repeated infection and inflammation, which in turn produces
recurrent cough and fever. This can be a life sentence, but it is
not a killer that gnaws and eats away the body; it is not consumption. No doubt Louis's illness, his bronchiectasis, dated
back to some childhood infection, such as whooping cough. He
would always be subject to attacks of cough and fever, but he
was not consumptive, and there was no danger to life. In any
case, it was as clear as can be that the main problem was nervous disorder; the cure would involve separating Louis from his
family for a reasonable period of time.

I am a practical man. I am happy to use the label of physical
disease as an alias for nervous disorder, if this will effect a cure.
Louis could be said to have a 'threatening' of consumption, to
coin a phrase which meant very little but which couldn't be dis-
puted. I would use this approach to justify my medical advice
that he should travel immediately to the south of France, and
that he should travel alone. This was the promise that I had
made to Louis when we had parted that afternoon, and I would
confirm it with a written opinion the very same evening.

As my carriage approached the house, the comforting glow
of the gas lamp on the corner of Cavendish Square came into
view through the rain. I reflected on the singular fact that I had
spent the entire journey thinking about Louis Stevenson: one
patient out of so many seen that day, and really not even ill, cer-

tainly not in comparison with the dying consumptive girl at the hospital. Louis was a young man who had achieved nothing worthwhile in his 22 years, but undoubtedly he had a personality that was both engaging and memorable. I determined to do whatever was in my power to help the aspiring author. The only worry on my mind as I stepped out of the carriage, home at last, was the inevitable wrath of Louis's formidable father.

Chapter Three

IT WAS EXACTLY ONE week since Louis's consultation at Cavendish Square. The Stevensons had responded to their son's letter and my written opinion by travelling down from Edinburgh at the earliest opportunity. They wanted an interview as soon as possible: there were many questions to be answered.

For my part, I was as busy as ever that day and I knew that my meeting with Louis's parents would be long and difficult. Although I am supposed to have a robust personality, I felt somewhat agitated at the prospect of explaining my opinion to them. I knew that they were waiting in the dining room, but I wasn't in a hurry to see them. My work, always methodical, became more deliberate. I am capable of procrastination at times such as this.

When eventually I could delay the meeting no longer, I went into the dining room to meet the Stevensons, as a gesture of apology for their long wait. After nearly three hours confined in the room, watching patients and relatives come and go, Mrs. Margaret Stevenson appeared distinctly pale. Her forehead glistened with sweat; her breathing was rapid, despite her attempts to control it. I feared that she would faint. Perhaps she had fainted earlier on but, if so, I had not been aware of any disturbance in the dining room; a patient or relative who faints while waiting to be seen usually succeeds in creating a scene of turmoil, effectively usurping control of the situation from the physician. Yet all had been quiet.

'I'm delighted to meet you, Mr. and Mrs. Stevenson, and I am so very sorry for the delay.' My manner was energetic and genial as I launched myself into an attempt at conquest. 'I'm afraid that you can't avoid noticing the passage of time in this room, with my clock chiming every quarter hour. It's a wonderful timepiece, though, presented to me by the Governors of The London Hospital at the end of the 1866 cholera epidemic. What a terrible time that was for us in the East End: so much suffering, so many deaths. Did you know that the outbreak was caused by an unfiltered water supply? And the Water Company was never prosecuted! Fortunately, it won't happen again, thanks to the new Sanitary Bill. Progress indeed, Mr. and Mrs. Stevenson, progress indeed.'

This flurry of words, delivered as it might have been to an audience at the theatre, no doubt disguised my nervousness. As I was speaking, however, it seemed to me that my important visitors might be less formidable, less aggressive, than I had feared.

Thomas Stevenson, florid, solid-looking, spoke in a friendly, respectful, professional-to-professional tone. 'Thank you for agreeing to see us at short notice, Dr. Clark. Of course, we know that you're a busy man, but you'll appreciate that we're very concerned about our son's health.' His jacket, coal-black, was fastened at the top button only, allowing a measure of freedom for his modest, waistcoated paunch.

And so we moved into my consulting room. Mrs. Stevenson, still pale, sat stiffly upright, her hands on her lap, fingers intertwined, fidgeting in slow motion. 'Louis didn't tell us that he was coming to London. This has been a great shock to us, especially to Tom. Our son's health has always been delicate, doctor. He's just not strong enough for unnecessary travelling.' She spoke quietly, but her words had the force of transparent sincerity. Good looking but not beautiful, her appearance was curiously enhanced and strengthened by her aquiline nose.

'Louis told us that he's been 'ordered south', doctor, and he described your orders as 'peremptory'. Of course, he's always had a weak chest but does all this mean something worse than we feared? If he's seriously ill, then surely it would be better for him to come home.' Her voice, rising in pitch, began to sound indignant.

I had expected any assault to come from Louis's father, not from his mother. On the defensive, I attempted to divert her attention towards mundane details of her son's medical history. In this way, I established that Louis had suffered repeated fevers and bronchial infection dating back to the croup illness in early childhood, and apparently becoming more prominent after a six week bout of whooping cough at the age of ten. There had been a number of episodes of 'bronchitis', 'influenza of the lungs' or 'pleurisy', usually during the winter or spring months. As I had suspected, there was nothing in the history to suggest consumption.

During her account of Louis's illnesses, Mrs. Stevenson produced some notes, with details dating back to her son's early life. I found it difficult to conceal my unease and irritation as I began to lose control of the interview. Written information from a patient or relative is not helpful. As far as I am concerned, such material disrupts my flow of leading questions with a tangle of irrelevant detail. I have no doubt that my expression darkens whenever a sheath of documents is slapped on my desk; still more when I see the hesitant production of a small piece of paper every inch of which is covered with tiny handwriting. Of course, my own extensive notes and written instructions to patients fall into a different category, representing a cornerstone of my professional reputation.

'I'm very grateful to you, Mrs. Stevenson, for the detailed information. I must make it clear at the outset that I didn't find any signs of disease when I examined Louis.'

'Then why has he been ordered south?' she asked, in some bewilderment.

'Well, let me put it this way.' I was aware that I was beginning to bluster. 'His frail condition suggests that there may be a threatening of disease.'

'A threatening of disease.' She repeated the phrase, looking anxiously at her husband.

'Yes, a threatening of disease.' I was speaking more rapidly. 'Of course, there is no way that we can look into a man's chest, but I suspect that Louis may have some lung lesions.'

'Lesions?' She wrinkled her nose and furrowed her forehead.

'Yes, lesions. This may be speculation. If so, then it is speculation based on considerable experience.' Stroking my beard, and speaking these words of self-justification, I was uncomfortably aware that I might be lapsing into pomposity. This is the role that I have to play; I don't say that it is easy or enjoyable.

'Dr. Clark, if Louis has lung lesions and a threatening of disease, then he needs looking after. He is my only child, and I'll do anything that is needed to help him. I am sure that Tom would agree to let me go to Menton, or wherever you recommend.' She hesitated, glancing at her husband before adding: 'but perhaps Torquay would be more convenient.'

I spoke gently, choosing my words with care. 'Mrs. Stevenson, I must tell you that there is an element of nervous disorder in your son's illness. He will recover if he has a few weeks away from home. I would also advise that he must follow my general directions and dietary instructions.' I passed her a handwritten diet sheet, hoping that she would concentrate on the mechanics of this, rather than question me about the nature of Louis's nervous disorder.

The instructions that I had written out were detailed and specific. Louis was to have breakfast between 8 and 9 o'clock: dry toast, fresh fish or fat (not lean) bacon, a large cup of tea (not infused for more than five minutes) – and so on, with precise orders for the whole day, including advice to go to bed at least an hour before midnight.

Mrs. Stevenson studied my carefully written, personalised notes. She looked interested. She looked impressed. However much my colleagues may laugh at such 'general directions', the fact remains that patients and their relatives invariably take them seriously. I stand or fall by what my patients think of me, and not by the opinions of other doctors.

There was silence as she read the details of the diet recommended for Louis. She leaned her head to one side and absently entangled the fingers of her right hand in the lace cravat that was tied loosely round her neck. After a few minutes, her husband, perhaps anxious that she would be blaming herself for some imagined deficiency in the management of family meals, moved the conversation into a different area.

'You referred to 'an element of nervous disorder', Dr. Clark. Perhaps Louis told you that there have been difficulties within the family during the last few months.'

I was surprised that he was prepared to discuss this sensitive subject. Perhaps the distinguished engineer was reassured by my middle-aged manner, or perhaps by my overt religious conviction (the words 'Glory to God' on the wall had not gone unnoticed). It appeared that he might be willing to confide in me.

'Yes,' I replied, 'that's part of the problem. His heart is in literature. It seems that other matters are a burden to him.'

Mr. Stevenson frowned. 'Literature can hardly be described as a career. Even Sir Walter Scott himself found it necessary to work as an advocate. Don't misunderstand me, Dr. Clark, I don't despise literature – far from it – and I appreciate that my son has the gift of a wonderful imagination, but Louis needs a profession: a hobby will not feed and clothe him.'

Needless to say, I agreed with Thomas Stevenson's material sentiments. Nevertheless, I felt that I had to support my patient's point of view.

'I understand that some of Louis's work has already been published.'

'If you mean *The Pentland Rising*, then the answer is yes, but this was privately printed at my expense. I encouraged Louis to write it. I didn't have anything in mind other than pride at seeing his name in print. That was all there was to it.'

'He was only 16 when he wrote that,' added Mrs. Stevenson, her face flushing and flowering into a smile. She half-closed her eyes, like a contented cat, and exhaled softly through her nose. 'And, Tom, we haven't told Dr. Clark that Louis has got an article coming out in the *Portfolio* soon, published under the pseudonym 'L.S. Stoneven': one of his little jokes. It's an essay called 'Roads', doctor, for which he will be paid three pounds and eight shillings.' She paused. 'Of course, that's less than the allowance that Tom gives him.'

I arched an eyebrow in enquiry, but my curiosity was not satisfied; there was no mention of the actual amount of the allowance.

Mr. Stevenson leaned towards his wife and held her hand. He was not afraid of showing affection for her in company.

'Maggie, we love him and we've spoilt him. Of course we've tried to limit his income to a sensible level, but he's never been genuinely short of money. Even now, he's driving round London in a hansom cab with no thought given to the expense. Has he never heard of omnibuses?'

Mrs. Stevenson, still holding her husband's hand, turned to me. 'Tom isn't really concerned about the expense, doctor, but he is concerned about Louis. He's always been devoted to his son, and so affectionate! When Louis had night-time fever, it was usually Tom who would sit by his bed and comfort him with stories. Tom had a nickname for him, Smoutie, which we used in the family until Louis was 15 or more. Don't you agree that there's a special friendship that can exist only between father and son? And Tom was so brave when Louis abandoned engineering. It was deeply disappointing, considering that Louis had just written a wonderful paper on lighthouses, but Tom showed no anger, and immediately offered to support him through a course of legal studies. No father could have done more for his son.'

'I can understand that all this must have been difficult for you, Mr. Stevenson, bearing in mind your professional responsibilities to the Northern Lighthouse Board.' I was eager to show respect for Louis's father, personifying as he did the revered tradition of lighthouse engineering.

'Difficult indeed,' he replied. 'My profession has been demanding in so many different and burdensome ways. I'm sure you can understand that. The years of study, the years of service under my brother in the construction of the Skerryvore lighthouse. The strains of partnership in the family firm, the countless hours spent preparing my contributions to scientific journals.

At the age of 55, I feel that I've been on a treadmill for most of my life. Of course, I couldn't have carried on without Maggie's devoted support, and neither of us could have achieved anything without our faith in God.'

I remained silent. He stood up and began pacing up and down, not in the jerky and frenetic style of his son, but slowly, with head bowed and expression stern.

'I suppose Louis told you of our dispute, arising from his outright rejection of our faith. Nothing could have been more calculated to wound me, and yet he seemed almost careless in his dismissal of our Lord Jesus Christ.' His voice was becoming stentorian, his facial colour puce. 'He said that he was simply being honest, but he must have known that his so-called honesty would destroy us as a family. I would rather see him dead than an atheist.'

Mrs. Stevenson, flustered, intervened. 'Of course Tom doesn't mean that, Dr. Clark, although we both feel deeply hurt by Louis's behaviour. After all, I'm a daughter of the manse and hardly likely to sympathise with atheism. Louis knows that I stand with Tom, and nothing will change that.'

Louis had told me: 'my mother is my father's wife'.

Mr. Stevenson, seated again, looked tired and vacant. Eventually, he spoke in a low, almost inaudible, voice.

'Perhaps I should be consulting you myself, doctor. The fact is that I can't work properly because my mind is distracted. I don't sleep for more than two or three hours, and I wake in a prison of despair. Louis has done this to me: this is my reward for all the tenderness that I've shown him over the years.'

I had an uneasy feeling that he might reveal too much of himself.

'Put away your fears, Mr. Stevenson. Remember that work

will see you through any difficulty. Our children will always test us, and perhaps destroy us if we let them do so; it's only natural that our love for them is greater than their love for us.'

My words had the desired effect of inhibiting any deeper insight into his anguish, and halting the descent into tears.

Mrs. Stevenson moved a hand towards her husband, gently touching his shoulder. 'Tom will fight on, Dr. Clark, but he's not as tough as people believe. Let me tell you this. When our Skye terrier Coolin was run over by a coach and killed four or five years ago, Tom just couldn't bear to look at the dog's body; it was Louis – our delicate son Louis – who brought home the body, dug the grave and laid Coolin in it. Tom has a sensitive nature. He may be ten years older than I am, but I have to be his mother as well as his wife.'

I smiled, pleased that I had allowed the Stevensons to talk to each other as much as to myself, and relieved that their questions had not been too searching. I had no doubt that Louis should go abroad, although sympathy for his parents had almost overridden my determination to help the young writer. Any attempt to keep the family together would surely result in a complete breakdown of Louis's nervous system. Thomas's nervous system might well break down anyway, but there did seem to be an element of enjoyment in his depression and perhaps that would protect him. I could only guess at the complex causation of Louis's separation from his loving father; I doubted that the religious dispute was anything more than an event that they could both conveniently blame.

At this point, I judged that I should bring the conversation back to Louis's physical condition. I picked up Mrs. Stevenson's piece of paper, which she had discreetly placed on my desk, and

I read through the careful summary of her son's childhood illnesses. It was not after all so very detailed, and perhaps it did show a pattern:

Spring 1853: Croup

Spring 1854: Fever and bronchitis

Summer 1854: Bronchitis

1856: Scarlet Fever

January-February 1857: Bronchitis

November 1857: Bronchitis (he spent his seventh birthday in bed)

January & May 1858: Bronchitis

September 1858: Gastric Fever

1859: Very delicate for the next few winters

1861: Whooping cough

1864: He had to leave Edinburgh Academy (too many colds)

February 1867: Pleurisy

1868: Influenza

1868: Bronchitis

There was also a record of her son's delirious, screaming night-time attacks, which had occurred repeatedly over several years.

I smoothed out the piece of paper on the desk in front of me. The thought crossed my mind that I shouldn't necessarily dismiss such contributions out of hand; I had to admit that this one was useful.

'May I keep this for my records, Mrs. Stevenson? It's certainly most helpful and, as a written medical history, it puts the efforts of many of my students to shame.'

She blushed, delightfully, like a young girl.

'Thank you, doctor, but I'm simply a loving mother. Louis is my only child. He needs me and I need him.'

'I must be honest with you,' I replied, with a little more force. 'It's true that his lungs are delicate, and vulnerable to disease. At the same time, paradoxically, he's more likely to regain health if he leaves the protection of your loving care for a period of time.'

Mr. Stevenson turned to face his wife.

'The doctor's orders are clear, Maggie. We'll have to let Louis go. Perhaps a six week break would be adequate.'

I didn't disagree, although I suspected that Louis, once he had escaped, might need some persuasion to come home.

There was silence as the Stevensons at last realised that they could not change my opinion. I was uncomfortably aware that they suspected me of being in league with their son. Perhaps their suspicion was not entirely unfounded; perhaps Louis had charmed and cajoled me into accepting his point of view. I am not a man who has either the time or the inclination to analyse the origins of my advice. I act intuitively, and I try to ensure that my manner has at least the appearance of untroubled self-confidence.

In this way, I played my role. On the fifth of November, Louis left London for Dover. On the next day, his parents journeyed home to Edinburgh. Much later, I learned that they had attended a service at St. Michael's Church in Paddington in which the clergyman had taken his text from the fourth chapter of the Gospel according to St. John: 'Go thy way; thy son liveth.'

Chapter Four

THE 1870S PASSED WITH accelerating speed as my day-to-day work continued its relentless course. It was only the growth of my children that marked one year from another, and, with six birthdays to remember or forget, even this was an unreliable indicator of the time that I had lost. Unlike Thomas Stevenson, I had no intention of allowing emotion or family dispute to jeopardise the balance of my mind; by working 16 hours a day, I was able to put aside thought in favour of the action of the moment. My life was set in a pattern that I believe will have to continue until disability brings me down. I depend on the intensity of my work to protect me from the demon of inner agitation, that senseless sense of foreboding which might otherwise destroy me.

During this time, my reputation and the demand for my services continued to grow. I have to say that this was in no small part the result of my association with Mr. Gladstone. After the Liberal government fell in 1874, Disraeli came to power as the Tory Prime Minister, and Gladstone moved out of the centre of government for a period of time, setting up house in Harley Street, conveniently close to Cavendish Square. Throughout the next five years, I attended my most important patient as and when needed, sometimes more than once a day; any symptom was taken seriously, and many prescriptions were written. It was during this time that our professional relationship matured into genuine friendship.

In 1876 I persuaded Gladstone to present prizes at the Medical

School. It was a wonderful occasion. Although I could not rival the great man's powerful, resonating speech I believe that I did make some impact with my description of the medical calling.

> The profession which you have chosen is one of the noblest, the most important and the most interesting of all those occupations to which the highest human endeavours are turned. But it is also the most self-denying and the most arduous; exacting the largest internal sacrifices, it returns the fewest external rewards.

This statement did not provoke laughter, despite my fame as one of the wealthiest physicians in Britain. For every medical man earning thousands of pounds a year in London, there are hundreds of doctors within and outwith the capital city who have difficulty in scraping together a modest income. And so the students at The London were forewarned: they should not expect to acquire their own Cavendish Square.

My greatest service to Gladstone came in July of 1880, soon after he had moved back to Downing Street as Prime Minister at the age of seventy. It was pneumonia, that most dangerous of diseases, which can strike with the suddenness of a knife attack, a moment when the temperature shoots up to transform a healthy body at ease with itself into a chilled and shaking mass of fear. For several days, the days of continuous high fever and anxiety, I visited my patient not only daily but at times on an hourly basis. And then, thank God, came the crisis, that dramatic fall in temperature, the transition to the state of comfort which signals recovery. I had taken the precaution of calling in Sir William Jenner, the Queen's physician, for a second opinion; if things had gone badly, if Gladstone had died, it would have been helpful to share the blame with such a distinguished colleague, but in the event I was happy to take the credit for the Prime Minister's recovery. My delight at his revival was manifest: I had established my credentials with the Gladstone family, and with the upper strata of society, beyond any doubt.

And so, by the end of the decade, my standing as a London physician was higher than it had ever been, and my Cavendish Square practice was at times almost under siege from patients demanding to see me. Despite this, I continued my regular attendance at The London Hospital, determined as I was to keep my knowledge of advanced disease up to date. In any case, the loyalty of this 'poor Scotch beggar' to the hospital made it certain that my carriage would continue to roll over the congested streets to Whitechapel for as long as I was needed.

I must now relate what happened to Louis Stevenson during these years; his life story is likely to be of more interest to the wider world than is mine. The information that I can give is necessarily limited: I saw him in April 1874, but then more than six years was to pass before he crossed the threshold of Cavendish Square again.

His visit in the spring of 1874, en route to Edinburgh from Menton after a stay of six months rather than six weeks, was a delightful occasion. He appeared well and in good humour, referring in a jokingly disparaging way to the English who populated Menton (or Mentone, as he insisted on pronouncing it, in the Italian manner, in recognition of the status of the town prior to its annexation by France a few years earlier). Apparently, Dr. Bennet had agreed with me that there were no signs of disease, and had cheerfully charged Louis 25 francs for this reassurance.

Worryingly, Louis had not followed my instructions precisely during that period of time. Staying in Paris on his way home from Menton, he had developed a cold, and had neglected to follow my detailed, written directions.

...as soon as you feel the first emanations of having caught a feverish cold, go at once to bed, cover yourself with bedclothes to encourage free perspiration, confine yourself to a slop or fever diet, and take a large teaspoonful of Solution of Citrate of Ammonia in an ounce of water every two hours until the feverishness subsides and the cough loosens. If the attack does not yield within twenty four hours, send for your medical adviser but continue the treatment until he sees you and prescribes afresh...

Fortunately, the cough had not progressed beyond mild bronchitis, perhaps indicating improved general health and better resistance to infection. A buoyantly optimistic Paris doctor had encouraged him with the opinion that, after all, he might have had something worse, such as smallpox.

It was soon after that spring of 1874 that Louis's essay 'Ordered South' appeared in *Macmillan's Magazine*. I read this with a curious sense of intimacy; I was the man who had given the 'order'. Needless to say, there was no reference to my name, nor to the circumstances of our meeting. Instead, there was introspection.

I dare say the sick man is not very inconsolable when he receives sentence of banishment, and is inclined to regard his ill-health as not the least fortunate accident of his life.

And I remembered that it was Louis himself who had instigated the 'order': I was simply the man who had added a signature.

As the decade progressed I tried to keep track of his publications, but it seemed that these were few and far between. A small book entitled *An Inland Voyage* surfaced in 1878: the record of a canoe journey made by Louis with his friend, the young baronet Sir Walter Simpson, from Antwerp to Pontoise. This was pleasant enough, and I was interested in the Simpson connection, knowing that Sir Walter was the son of the first baronet, Sir James Young Simpson, the man who had been professor of midwifery in Edinburgh during my time as an anatomy student there. It was Sir James who had developed and championed the use of chloroform as an anaesthetic in childbirth, eventually achieving recognition and indeed triumph with its use at the birth of the Queen's son, Prince Leopold, in 1853. Sir James was a man whose name will still be remembered and revered a hundred years hence.

My reading of *An Inland Voyage* suggested that the young Stevenson and the young Simpson were, not surprisingly, less serious and less substantial than their respective, respectable fathers. Why was one of the canoes named *Cigarette*? And did the concluding sentence – 'the most beautiful adventures are not those we go to seek' – represent some kind of personal statement by Louis?

Another small book, *Travels with a Donkey in the Cévennes*, was published the next year. This came to my attention through the columns of the *Spectator*, a magazine with the curious and inexplicable property of producing addiction to its pages. An anonymous reviewer claimed that the book revealed 'a susceptibility towards the softer sex', as if this was in some way a disability.

> Until a man has passed out of the stage when women, with their love and their charms, make up all religion to

him, his judgement on the intellectual beauty of different creeds is worth as little as his love.

For my own part, I found the review more difficult to read than the book, which was charming and thought-provoking, with intriguing hints of personal unhappiness. But there was something more: as I turned the pages, time and again I felt that Louis was in harmony with the state of my mind.

To hold a pack upon a pack-saddle against a gale out of the freezing north is no high industry, but it is one which serves to occupy and compose the mind. And when the present is so exacting, who can annoy himself about the future?

Precisely! Nothing is better than the action of the moment for banishing thought and worry.

These books were enjoyable enough to read during my carriage journeys to and from the hospital. But I have to say that, by October 1880, when Louis was expected again at 16 Cavendish Square, my pleasure at the thought of seeing him was tarnished by disappointment: disappointment that he had produced such a meagre literary output since I had 'ordered' him to go south. I felt a powerful sense of personal involvement in his case, and I remembered him with an unusual clarity of image. I needed to know why this ambitious author, now aged nearly thirty, had made so little impact on the world of books. I needed to know if Louis's medical condition was the cause of his slow progress. I needed to know if I should adjust my diagnosis of 1873. If a physician is to protect his reputation, then it is necessary for him to review every case from time to time.

Chapter Five

IT WAS LIKE A meeting of old friends. Although I hadn't seen Louis for more than six years, I had no difficulty in recognising the slender, active figure. He was shown into the study by Reynolds, the butler who had belittled the young law student in 1873. Somewhat scruffily dressed, and still with shoulder length hair, Louis's appearance was dominated, even more than before, by his gleaming, almost luminous, brown eyes which immediately fixed on me with an expression of dependency.

'My dear Dr. Clark, did I ever thank you enough for getting me abroad all those years ago? I can assure you that, since then, I've never failed to sing the praises of my champion doctor to anyone who cared to listen. You're a trump. Without your help, I doubt that I'd have survived with my sanity intact.'

Involuntarily, I beamed. I was surprised how pleasantly flattered I felt by these words of praise from a young man whose good opinion was hardly necessary to a professional man of my well-established reputation.

Louis was not alone. He was accompanied by a figure with an appearance almost as compelling as his own: his wife, Fanny. A clear gaze, a strong face, a swarthy complexion, wavy and very black hair; small hands, well used to work, short nails. She spoke with a twangy, American accent.

'I haven't come to say anything, Dr. Clark, but I'd like to hear what you have to say.'

Her words, friendly enough in themselves, seemed to carry a

vague threat. I thought it likely that she would in fact have something to say to me – something more testing – before the interview was finished.

For the time being, it was easier for me to talk of literature than of medical matters. 'Of course, I've tried to keep up with anything published under the name of Stevenson.'

Louis smiled. 'That won't have occupied much of your time. I can't claim to have produced more than a couple of books and a handful of essays, but believe me when I say that I have written something every day that my health has allowed.'

I eagerly offered my good opinion of *An Inland Voyage* and *Travels with a Donkey*.

'Thank you, doctor.' The author's mock graciousness didn't disguise his pleasure. 'It's a pity that the critics didn't have the same view. They couldn't find anything of interest in *Inland Voyage*. You can imagine my disappointment at that: my first book, the book that for many months I would handle, caress even, with a luxurious feeling of contentment, simply because of its existence in print. And *Travels with a Donkey* was savaged – anonymously of course – in the columns of 'Grandmama' *Spectator*; I was accused of dwelling on matters of love as if this was a fault or even a crime. In my own defence, I have to say that the book was written after I'd parted from Fanny, a parting that we thought might be for ever. I suppose I was influenced by the sadness of that time. Can you blame me for that?'

'Of course not, Louis. And I can assure you that no one likes criticism.' Unusually for me, I slipped easily into Christian name address; after all, Louis was about the same age as my eldest son.

'I take it that you gave up your law studies to pursue a career in literature.'

'I did indeed, but not abruptly. After I'd seen you, I returned home resolved to improve relations with my parents. My mother suspected that your opinion had been a put up job to allow me to escape, but she was happy enough that I was home again. My father and I agreed to differ on matters of religion, and we decided – amicably, and with mutual respect – that I should complete my law studies in Edinburgh. You'll be surprised to learn that I passed the final examination for the Scottish Bar the very next year. My father, hoping to nail me to an Advocate's life, fixed a brass plate with my name on to the door of our house in Heriot Row. But I had to disappoint him again. I made the fateful decision to devote my life to literature, and I retired from the law with my total earnings at less than ten pounds. So you see me here today: an author in search of a living.'

I stroked my beard. 'Today' was five years after Louis's remarkably early retirement from the legal profession, and by his own admission his earnings from literature during that time must have been minimal.

'And your health, Louis. What about your health?'

'A few bad colds during my time at home, and the usual problems with catarrh: a wonderfully ugly word that, isn't it, but don't challenge me to spell it. There was nothing really serious during those years. You already know about my canoe journey in France and Belgium; I think you'll agree that wasn't a bad effort for a so-called invalid. And in the winter before that I managed to complete a long, lone walk (70 miles, my mother reckons) in Galloway. I was in my finest exercisy state then, as fit as a fiddle, and of course I wrote an article about my adventure.'

'So you didn't need much medical attention at that time?'

'There hasn't been any time when I've failed in my duty to

support the medical profession, but it's true that I didn't need much treatment then. On just a few occasions I had to resort to taking opium at night. It was a wonderful way of transforming my hacking cough into tranquil euphoria and strange dreams: altogether preferable to the unmitigated terror of my childhood nightmares. I haven't made a habit of opium, though, I reserve that for my beloved cigarettes.'

I nodded in acquiescence. I was confident that Louis could be counted amongst the readership of De Quincey, and therefore he would be aware of the pains of opium as well as its pleasures. As far as I am concerned, opium remains my greatest ally in relieving the suffering of others; there are some forms of agony which, if unrelieved, would go beyond the limits of human tolerance.

'After my *Inland Voyage* was completed,' Louis went on, 'I spent a good deal of my time in France, mainly Paris and the neighbourhood of Fontainebleau. Fortunately for me I met Fanny at Grez-sur-Loing in 1876. As you see, we are now a stately married couple.'

Fanny, sitting bolt upright, took this as her cue to join in the conversation.

She snorted. 'Hardly a stately married couple yet, but we'll get there. My first meeting with Louis, Dr. Clark, was four years ago, as he says. I'm sure I remember it better than he does. That skinny figure jumping in through the window of the hotel room to the applause of the diners: it was a scene that's now a part of me, fixed in my mind with the clarity and colour of a magic lantern slide. But that was four years ago, and it hasn't been plain sailing in the meantime. You'll understand why when I tell you that I'm fully ten years older than Louis: first married when I was 16, and divorced only a few months ago, with a 12-year-old son in tow and a 22-year-old daughter back home. I'm sure you'll agree that it's not exactly a story book marriage for Louis.'

It took a good deal of self-control to restrain the gasp of astonishment that so nearly escaped from me as I listened to her words. My mind leapt immediately and with sympathy to Louis's parents: how had they handled this extraordinary turn of events? Surely Louis's father, that stalwart of Calvinism, couldn't have accepted the marriage without strong resistance, and surely this resistance must have been as agonising as the earlier dispute for Louis. And yet Fanny's manner was in no way apologetic: she would not release me from her gaze while she was speaking. 'You'll understand that our marriage was not encouraged by others.'

My train of thought was diverted to my own first marriage, that ideal match between a Royal Navy surgeon and an officer's daughter. She came with a dowry of £500 a year, and let no one despise me for valuing that, unless they themselves have refrained from such calculations. It was such a good marriage, and it was certainly encouraged by others. Her death and my remarriage have not taken her away; I doubt that a day will ever pass without her image joining me in thought, and at that level the mind does not distinguish between the living and the dead.

Louis, fidgeting, needed to join in. 'Fanny is no ordinary woman, doctor. I needn't bother you with descriptions of her rascally husband – her first husband, I mean – but you'll get some idea of Fanny's toughness when I tell you that she left him in California and brought her three children to Europe in 1875, so that she could study painting, with only a small allowance to live on, and no one to turn to for help.'

'Three children?'

'Yes, three children,' answered Fanny, 'including my little son Hervey, who was only four years old when we arrived in Antwerp. My mind and energies were taken up with survival; our rooms were primitive, even by my standards, and I've lived in some pretty rough places in California, I can tell you. And to cap it all, it turned out that the Academy was closed to women; I wasn't a man, and therefore I wasn't allowed to learn about painting. You might say that I should have checked this out before leaving America, but it never occurred to me that I would be debarred from studying because of my womanhood. Such are the mysteries of academic institutions. And then, as if I hadn't got enough to worry about, I was hit by the worst blow of all: my little Hervey fell ill. Burning fever every night, and the doctor hadn't a clue what was wrong with him. That was the reason I uprooted my family again and moved to Paris: it was to get help for Hervey. At least we found a better doctor, an American, but the little boy got sicker despite all the medicine that was prescribed. The doctor gave him quinine and more quinine, but the fever got worse and worse. It was consumption, scrofulous consumption. His neck was a mass of glands, all sticking out, with the skin broken down and foul. His belly was swollen and tense, and yet his limbs were as puny as twigs: his body was melting into a skeleton before my eyes. And despite everything – his fever, his diarrhoea, his convulsions, his bleeding – little Hervey was so brave. For weeks, I hardly left his side, and I suffered with him in a way which no one but a mother could understand. When he died, and we followed his tiny coffin to the cemetery at St. Germain, it wasn't a relief. I wanted him to live, I still want him, and yet all I have left of him is the memory of his suffering.'

Her absolutely steady voice and the absence of tears invested her words with emotional power. I was disconcerted by my reaction: my eyes were perceptibly moist, and I do believe that I could have wept if I had allowed myself to do so.

There was silence for a few moments before Louis spoke.

'It wasn't until the following year that we met. After that, I spent as much of my time as possible in France. I now look back on 1877 as an idyllic year for Fanny and myself, but it was a false dawn: the next year Sam, her husband, demanded that she should return to California, and off she went. That's why *Travels with a Donkey*, which I wrote in the aftermath of her departure, was in one sense a long letter to Fanny, despite being officially dedicated to Professor Colvin.'

'It wasn't just a question of being sent for and going,' interjected Fanny. 'I was dependent on Sam for what little money I had. In any case, I needed time to think, and I needed to get my daughter Belle away from the attentions of a knavish suitor. Louis doesn't understand that responsibility for a 20-year-old daughter can weigh heavily on a mother.'

I tried to convey my sympathy with a knowing look. As the father of two daughters from my first marriage, I was able to achieve this without difficulty.

Fanny leaned forward, her dress rustling. It was a black dress, curiously mismatched with a maroon jacket, and in startling contrast with bright, white stockings, occasionally glimpsed below the hemline. Her cravat, also white, was tied too tightly. It was the attire of a woman with no interest in fashion.

She became more energetic in her speech as she went on. '1877 wasn't entirely idyllic, anyway, Louis. Remember that you had a bad cold in September, and I had to bring you to London to get treatment for your eye infection.'

'Eye infection?' I asked, conscious that Louis's medical history was becoming increasingly submerged in the conversation between husband and wife.

It was Louis who answered. 'More than a bad cold, I should say. It was a complication of influenza. Personally, I blame the French doctor who advised me to irrigate my nostrils with salt water. From my point of view, it was nothing less than a punishing exercise in nasal gymnastics. Yes, I'd forgotten that unpleasant incident, but I certainly remember our return to London the next summer. We lodged in Chelsea: it was just a small boarding house, quite a come down from the Paddington Hotel where I'd stayed on my visit to see you back in 1874. It was the last stop for Fanny before she went to Liverpool for the Atlantic crossing.'

All this was interesting enough, but I had not yet been told how Louis and Fanny came to be married. I spoke with a buoyancy that was intended to move the conversation onwards. 'A sad parting, no doubt. Leading, however, to *Travels with a Donkey*. Perhaps it was the seed of literary growth.'

'Too kind, dear Dr. Clark,' replied Louis. 'The fact is that, after *Travels with a Donkey*, I spent the next year producing very little – just a few essays, a few short stories, an attempt at a play – despite working for several hours a day at my writing. At the time, I thought that this must be the low point of my life, a period of despair with no end in sight. I yearned to break free from dependency on my father, and yet £30 for *Travels with a Donkey* was the best return for my work that I could muster. If only he'd criticised my work it would have been easier to bear than his loving kindness, his anxiety for my welfare, his prudence in all matters, his tight rein on my finances. 'Crabbed Age and Youth', doctor: published in *Cornhill Magazine*, but in reality a dart aimed at my father. 'Old and young, we are all on the same cruise – if there is a fill of tobacco among the crew, for God's sake pass it round, and let us have a pipe before we go!' Yes, I wrote it: a plain enough message, I think you'll agree. I look back on it now with a sense of shame.'

I wriggled uneasily on the seat of my leather chair. It didn't seem to occur to Louis that I was more likely to identify with his father's attitude of mind than with his own. And I was not comfortable with his careless use of the expression 'for God's sake'.

'Strong words indeed, Louis, but I can see that your father might not want you to use up all his tobacco. In any case, I've no doubt that the £30 you earned for your book must have had a sweeter taste than ten times that amount handed to you by your father.'

'That's true. It's certainly more painful to receive charity than to give it. I had to live with this. Much of my time at our home in Heriot Row last year was spent in solitude and in silence. I couldn't explain to my people the depth of my feelings for Fanny and, in any case, it seemed that she'd left me for good and all. You can imagine how I came back to life when she sent me a telegram, summoning me to California: she was ill, I had to go. I knew my parents would be horrified by this venture and I couldn't ask them for more money. I couldn't even tell them face to face where I was going. It was the day that I was supposed to be travelling on holiday with them to Cumberland. I met them on the train, and told them I was called away on business, leaving them to discover later that I'd gone to America. Such cowardice on my part, and the second time I'd done this to them. My dear father and mother, to whom I owe so much, and yet I was afraid to tell them about the woman I love. I was determined to free myself from financial dependency on my father, to make my living by writing and to marry Fanny.'

Fanny leaned forward, resting her hands on my desk.

'That was over a year ago, doctor, and now he's back home. What we need to know is, how on earth are we going to save him from his consumption?'

Chapter Six

CONSUMPTION. A WORD, with its second syllable emphasised. A word, meaning wasting away. A word, producing a physical reaction: warm blood filling my face with the irresistible force of a rapidly rising tide. However many times I may have heard this word, I still prefer to skirt round it, to use an alternative term. For many years, my own experience with tuberculosis stained me with guilt: the guilt of the unclean, diseased physician. Louis and Fanny were not to know this, but it was only six years earlier that I had suffered a relapse, long after I had considered myself freed from the disease. I can still recall all too easily my revulsion at the sight of the blood that I coughed up, the blood that I should have harboured in my veins. The frustrating idleness and the necessary period of leave from my hospital duties were detestable to me. But I recovered, and the intensity of my work for the most part suppressed my fear of further relapse, despite daily reminders at the hospital of the existence of tuberculosis. Yet the word consumption retains the power to strip away my veneer of composure.

Louis seemed to read my mind as he spoke. 'How I hate the word consumption.'

'Maybe,' replied Fanny, 'but we have to face the truth. I knew it when we were in Paris, and I was proved right by events in America. Anyway, consumption is not an incurable disease. That's the important thing. I'm sure Dr. Clark will agree.'

To be given the diagnosis, or the assumed diagnosis, without an opportunity to assess the evidence for it, is anathema to me. In effect, Fanny had destroyed my careful attempt to dissect the medical history and reach a logical conclusion. And yet her determination to fight on Louis's behalf was obvious, and had to be harnessed in the best interests of his treatment.

I managed to produce a smile which may or may not have disguised my irritation. 'I need to know what happened in America, Louis.'

'After I'd slipped away from my parents, I left within the week for New York. I had a second cabin berth on ss *Devonia*; not first class, because I needed to get away from the idea that I could be a first class passenger in life, and not steerage either, because I needed the luxury of a table to write on. I paid eight guineas for my passage, two guineas more than the steerage fare, but the food wasn't anything special: porridge every day, sometimes Irish stew, sometimes meat left over from the saloon, and – twice a week, I think, on pudding days – something resembling plum pudding. Even during such a short period of time, I learnt much of human nature from the steerage types, and I tried to be a generally agreeable companion. Certainly, my skill in rolling cigarettes was greatly admired and much in demand. I scribbled away at my notes, and later wrote it all up under the title of *The Amateur Emigrant*. I flatter myself that it makes a good story but I doubt that it'll see the light of day; my father hates the idea of his son as a steerage type, and wants it withdrawn from publication.'

'An exciting adventure, no doubt. I speak as an ex-Royal Navy surgeon, although I was never afloat. Perhaps the greatest joy of your voyage was the thought that it would be over within ten days or so.'

'Unfortunately,' replied Louis, 'there was worse to come. When I arrived in New York, I was plagued by itch, probably acquired from my new found friends in steerage. An apothecary said it was my liver, and gave me a blue pill, a powder and some colourless fluid to take. By the time I realised that his medicines were useless, I was travelling west on the railroad. It was a journey that I wouldn't wish to repeat: nothing to eat, and the train so crowded that I couldn't lie down. I just sat there, itching and scratching. My only relief was from a small supply of laudanum that I had with me, and it was this that finally allowed me to get some sleep as we were crossing Nebraska.'

Laudanum – tincture of opium in alcohol – that remedy for so many ills. Just a few drops can make the difference between discomfort and ease. A physician who could not wield this weapon of war against suffering would indeed be enfeebled. If I was forced to choose just one drug that I could continue to use for the benefit of my patients, then that drug would undoubtedly be laudanum, with its wonderful capacity for spreading around pain like warm treacle, closing it off with a coat of sweetness.

Fanny, sitting on the edge of her chair, her hands clenched and half outstretched towards me, needed to add words of explanation to Louis's account. 'Believe me, Dr. Clark, crossing America on the East-West railroad is not an experience to be recommmended at the best of times, and Louis was really much too frail to undertake the journey. But my own first trip across the continent from home in Indianapolis to join Sam in California was even more hair-raising. That was in 1864, before the railroad over to the west was built: I had to go east to New York, travel by steamer to Panama, cross the isthmus by rail, and then take another steamer to California. And I had my daughter Belle with me, a little girl only six years old then.'

Louis grinned, talking to me, looking at Fanny. 'You see that my wife is made of tough mettle, and she has a pioneering spirit. It is my great good fortune that, for some reason, she loves me and is prepared to look after this poor carcass of mine.'

'Were you ill when you arrived in California?' I asked.

'I wasn't well. My itchy rash still tormented me and, worse than that, I had to separate from Fanny soon after we'd been reunited in Monterey: the lawyer insisted on this until her divorce was finalised. And so I was alone in Monterey, waiting for Fanny's release. It was a time of depression and despair, not helped by pleading messages from my mother to return home. You can imagine how a telegram with the stark message 'Father desperately ill' would upset me, even though I didn't believe it. I couldn't respond because I had to wait for Fanny, and I was unwell myself. I'd lost a stone in weight during the three weeks of my journey to California, and then soon afterwards I developed pleurisy, out of the blue, without the usual cold to set it off. It was back to my old habit of fever, with a pulse of 150 and drenching sweats. I was living in the home of a little French doctor, who looked after me and dosed me up with tincture of aconite, but the whole business was bitterly disappointing. After all, it was the first time for several years that I'd needed to retreat to bed for a few days.'

Fanny joined in. 'I'd moved to Oakland by this time, Dr. Clark, to await my divorce from Sam, which was finalised in January. Even then, it was too soon for Louis and I to live together, but at least he was able to move to San Francisco, to be closer to me. He rented a room, and somehow survived from day to day. We were able to meet twice a week at a restaurant, which Louis couldn't really afford.'

'I confess that I wasn't eating much at that time, Fanny, but I wasn't well enough to write anything worthy of payment. I had to cut down my lunch expenditure from 50 cents to 25 cents. I even had to sacrifice my daily half-bottle of wine, which in any case was much less than I would have liked. I couldn't afford to use an oil lamp, and had to read and write by candlelight. You know well enough that I was never any good at sums, and it's not surprising that I got muddled with my money.'

'Not surprising, Louis, considering that you didn't even keep a record of the cheques that you were writing out. Only the son of a wealthy man could have allowed himself to acquire such bad habits.'

Louis gave a self-deprecating smile. 'You're right, of course, and I did have offers of money from my people, but only if I returned home. My pride wouldn't allow that, especially after I heard a rumour that my father had accused me of being a sponger. I've never felt more distant from him than I did at that time.'

'Louis was still feverish then; the doctor reckoned it was malaria, which I suppose he could have picked up on his journey through the mid-West. At any rate, quinine got his fever down, and at least Louis felt that he was getting some real medicine.'

'My best medicine, Dr. Clark, was my engagement to be married to the woman I'd loved for over three years. I confess, though, that I was skeleton thin, with my weight down to seven stone and falling, a good deal lighter than when I stepped on your scales for the first time seven years ago.'

It was then Fanny's turn to continue the tale. 'I was so worried about him that I moved him to a room at the Tubbs Hotel, so that I could call and see him more often. Too expensive for us I guess, but it was beginning to look like a matter of life and death.'

Louis, more animated now, was out of his chair, pacing around the room, emphasising each word with cutting and scything movements of his arms, his eyes shining, his hair flopping over his forehead.

'The Tubbs Hotel, March 1880, will be for ever etched on my memory. Feverish again, coughing, unable to eat, unable to work. And then something happened, something that had never happened before: I coughed up blood. I can't describe the despair I experienced when I tasted that blood. It had the flavour of death.'

Fanny's voice cut in, loud and at the same time confidential. 'I was desperately anxious about him, doctor, so much so that I moved him in to live with me at Sam's house, despite knowing that this would cause a scandal. Poor Louis, exhausted by fever and hacking cough, was unable to speak for much of the time. He was too weak to take proper nourishment: I kept him alive with hot fluids. By good fortune, we obtained the services of a wonderful doctor – William Bamford, an Englishman – who at first thought that Louis's time was up. He said that the weight loss, the fever, the cough and the blood spitting added up to galloping consumption. Not that he needed to tell me that. I knew already, had known it all along: it was my little Hervey's illness all over again. Louis was so brave when he coughed up blood, but all I could hear was the voice of Hervey crying for help. For me, it was a nightmare revisited, and yet, for as long as I had an ounce of strength left in my body, I wasn't going to let Louis die.'

'She fought ferociously to keep me going, and I could feel her strength seeping into me. You wouldn't have believed that this was the same woman who had been almost stuporous with depression only a few months earlier, when she had sent for me to come to her. She gave me the will to live at a time when I could so easily have given up the ghost.'

'Louis's fever began to settle. Dr. Bamford, who was so kind to us, thought that he might save him after all. By the end of March, we knew that Louis was going to survive, that he was going to live to write more books, to be a great author.'

Louis was now seated again, but restless as a five-year-old boy. 'Fanny would never have forgiven me if I'd died. After all, she'd just got a divorce to enable us to get married, and so I really couldn't disappoint her. Fanny saved me and Dr. Bamford was her faithful ally, calling daily to see his impoverished patient. As soon as I was well enough, I gave him a copy of *Travels with a Donkey*, inscribed with my thanks for his kindness and skill without which it would have been my last book. I trust that the sentiment was visible through the words. Dollars would have been preferred to my book, no doubt, but the doctor accepted the gift with good grace.'

'You'll realise, of course, that Louis's poverty was self-inflicted. It was only his stupid pride that prevented him from asking his father for money. I knew what had to be done. I wrote secretly to his parents and told them about Louis's illness, and about our marriage plans; I simply told them the truth.'

'She did the right thing, Dr. Clark. All my resentment dissolved when I received that marvellous telegram from my father: 'Count on £250 annually'. I was a child again, weeping at the depth of my parents' love for me, and of mine for them. I knew that they would save me and accept Fanny as my wife. Within a month, we were married in San Francisco; there were only two witnesses present, and everything was completed within a few minutes, but it was a truly auspicious day. I prophesy that the solidity of our marriage will in time be envied by many a couple joined together at grand cathedral ceremonies.'

Flattered as I was by Louis and Fanny's willingness to talk to each other using me as a non-speaking intermediary, I felt that I should inject a few words into the conversation. 'Congratulations, indeed, to both of you and, Louis, I can deduce simply from your appearance that your health has improved since then.'

'The money helped,' he replied. 'I could afford new teeth, which made my face look less startling, and we were able to go on honeymoon to the hills of California, above the Napa Valley.'

'A honeymoon on limited means,' added Fanny, 'but at least it was in the mountains, which I knew would be good for Louis's health. It was a ramshackle cabin in the Silverado mining camp, and once again I had to be carpenter as well as cook and everything else. Not what you'd call a luxurious honeymoon: we had to dig a pool to collect water, we had to use hay for our bunks, and we had only the cheapest of candles for our lighting. Anyway, we survived and, more than that, Louis got better. I knew that, because he was writing. One day in the not too distant future you'll be able to read all about us: *The Silverado Squatters*.'

'Well, yes, you'll be able to read all about us if I finish off the writing part of the job, and that can be a slow process, even when I'm working at it for five hours a day. I should be more productive, really, considering that I'm so much more settled in my mind now, a married man with a loving wife, and wonderfully reconciled with my parents.'

'We arrived in Liverpool just a couple of months ago: Louis, my son Lloyd and myself. Louis's friend Sidney Colvin came out on the tug to greet us, and Mr. and Mrs. Stevenson were waiting for us at the Northwestern Hotel. It was a welcome out of my dreams. Mr. Stevenson was charm itself, a man of courtesy and with a real sense of humour: not nearly so stern as I'd expected, and with something of the child in him. He loved it when I got round to addressing him as 'Master Tommy'. And Louis's mother was so happy to see her son, and so generous to me, plying me with gifts and treating me with the greatest respect. They'd obviously made up their minds to forgive Louis and to welcome me as their daughter-in-law. As soon as I met them I knew for sure that Louis's future – our future – would be as safe as they could possibly make it.'

Louis half closed his eyes; for a moment, it was his mother's face, shining with contentment. 'It was a great relief to me that Fanny got on so well with my parents. She even persuaded me that we should all go on a family holiday. I could have told her that summer in Scotland doesn't always seem like summer – you know that – but I confess that the beauty of the Highlands was more apparent to me on this visit than ever before. My parents were delighted with our company, and it was a delight that was both infectious and gratifying. The only drawback for me was my old enemy, the chronic cough.'

'What about the crowd in the hotel at Strathpeffer?' asked Fanny. 'You see, doctor, Louis took an instant dislike to our fellow guests, and only managed to relieve his feelings by writing a poem about them; he called it 'On Some Ghastly Companions at a Spa'. He's happier staying here in London at the Grosvenor Hotel but it's a mighty extravagant week, I can tell you.'

'Not surprising, really,' added Louis. 'Entertaining my literary friends at the Savile Club didn't come cheap, and I never could resist good Burgundy. Maybe the Napa Valley is the region of the future for wine, Dr. Clark, but for the time being I think you'll agree that nothing can compete with a fine Burgundy.'

I could hardly agree with his point of view. Even at that stage, I was something of a campaigner for temperance. My observations at the hospital have convinced me that alcohol rots the body and addles the mind. The strength of will needed for abstinence is, in my opinion, good for the soul. Louis's rather frivolous remarks about wine produced an involuntary, momentary, compression of my lips, but doubtless this was concealed by my moustache and beard. I trust that my voice was even in tone. 'I believe that drink is the enemy of the race, Louis, although I don't claim to be a total abstainer.'

There was a brief period of silence before Fanny spoke.

'I'll try to get Louis to moderate his taste for wine, doctor, and I think that'll be easier after we've left London. His literary friends, particularly Mr. Henley, are not necessarily a good influence on him. I've made strenuous efforts to be polite to them, despite knowing that they all opposed Louis's trip to America and his marriage to me. No doubt he's happy in their company, but it won't be them sitting at his bedside night and day when he starts coughing up blood again. The truth is that I can be more use to Louis and to his career than all his literary friends put together.'

Louis laughed. 'She's right, of course, and that's why she's here with me today. We've been sent to see you by my uncle, George Balfour, who as well as being my uncle happens to be a physician at Edinburgh Royal Infirmary: an eminent physician, I've heard it said. Uncle George, after listening to my chest, pronounced that I should travel to the mountains of Switzerland for treatment. Needless to say, Dr. Clark, this depends on your judgement. Could I be cured by going to Davos?'

And so with a simple, optimistic question, Louis placed responsibility for this fateful decision in the hands of the physician who had been his ally and co-conspirator seven years earlier, namely myself.

Chapter Seven

MY CAREFUL PHYSICAL EXAMINATION did not reveal any surprises. Although Louis had gained some weight since the nadir of the American adventure, he still appeared unnaturally thin. The outline of his ribs was clearly visible, separating furrows of sunken flesh, giving him a skeletal appearance that was exaggerated by his long, tapering fingers. I found no enlargement of neck glands, no abnormal abdominal mass. Listening to the chest with my stethoscope revealed a few deviant crackly sounds, but no sign of lung cavities.

After the examination had been completed, and whilst Louis was getting dressed up behind the screens which discreetly shielded him, I sat at the desk making notes. The silence was interrupted only by the squeak of nib on paper as I entered up my findings in a light blue ink on lined paper, occasionally changing my pen to use the red ink reserved for recording important findings or making small diagrams. I wrote more slowly than usual, giving myself time to consider the best way that I could present the facts to Louis and his wife.

When he was again seated opposite me, I leaned forwards towards him, with my elbows resting on the desk and my hands pressed together, almost as if in prayer. I contracted my face into an expression of earnest tension.

'The first thing to say, Louis, is that you can't have galloping consumption, simply because that condition is rapidly progressive and your condition is, if anything, improving.'

Louis smiled, but it was Fanny who replied.

'You should have seen him in America, doctor, when he was really ill. He may look thin now, but the loss of flesh over there was something different. Dr. Bamford stated categorically that it was galloping consumption.'

I could sympathise with Dr. Bamford, who had been faced with an apparently dying patient and the urgent need to provide Fanny with a diagnosis, some sort of explanation for what was happening. Death of a loved one is easier to face when the name of the enemy is known.

'Of course, I wasn't there and I can't put myself in Dr. Bamford's position, but perhaps the weight loss resulted from starvation. Louis simply wasn't eating enough to maintain his weight, and this in itself would make him vulnerable to illness. And don't forget that worry can also cause loss of weight.'

'Yes, I can confirm that I was worried, and I can also confirm that I was up and down the fever chart and spitting blood.'

'Any doctor would have suspected consumption, Louis' I replied. 'After all, and with apologies to your feelings, I probably don't need to tell you that the disease causes tens of thousands of deaths each year in this country alone. It's a plague the world over, and we all know that the combination of blood-spitting, fever and weight loss most likely means tuberculosis of the lungs.'

Immediately, I regretted speaking so plainly and so directly, without bothering to obscure my meaning with the cloud of verbosity which some colleagues regard as my trademark. Louis's lower lip trembled slightly and the corners of his mouth turned down: the child's harbinger of tears.

'On the other hand,' I continued, quickly, 'those symptoms

can have other meanings, and you need to remember that there is no way we can prove a diagnosis of consumption.' I was going to add 'during life', but checked myself short of this unnecessary honesty.

'Are you saying that Louis doesn't have consumption?' asked Fanny. 'If so, then why are we planning to go to Davos?'

'I'm not saying that. I'm simply trying to keep an open mind. Have you ever heard of a condition called bronchiectasis?'

'No,' replied Louis, 'and I don't think that I want a disease which has such a long and ugly name. I could never learn to spell it, let alone love it.'

'It's a condition in which the bronchi, the airways of the lungs, become widened and distorted by infection in childhood. These misshapen airways become inflamed, and that produces cough and spit, sometimes with blood, and sometimes with a lot of blood. From time to time, and this can be throughout adult life, you get attacks of fever, shivering and night sweats.'

Louis grimaced, and pushed his chair backwards, putting a little more distance between us. 'It sounds remarkably unpleasant. Are you sure that it wouldn't be better to have consumption?'

'Bronchiectasis is unpleasant, but not nearly so bad as consumption. The problem is that we can't always tell one from the other. I myself recognise ten points of difference between the two conditions, but my colleagues don't necessarily accept the truth of what I say. Not so long ago, I was accused in print, by a young physician from Leeds, of 'serving old wine in old bottles', and I don't think that he was referring to fine Burgundy.'

Louis yelped with laughter, apparently delighted with my attempt at humour. I was glad to have pleased him, but I should explain that I regard jokes as invariably irksome and often pointless.

'So what you're saying, doctor, is that I might have this bronchi-whatsit, and that I'm not dying of consumption after all.'

Fanny was not willing to let this pass without interjecting her own comments. 'Now hang on. Dr. Clark says that it's not always easy or even possible to tell the difference between the two. He also says that he can't put himself in Dr. Bamford's place and relive those terrible days in California. I saw that with my own eyes, and I know what consumption looks like. And consumption can sometimes be cured, can't it?'

In general, I believe that it is unwise to use the word 'cure'; disease has a habit of striking back. I paused and scratched my nose before replying. 'Consumption sometimes cures itself, and we can certainly give it a helping hand.'

She raised her right hand, like a schoolgirl in class, or perhaps she was pointing a finger at me. 'Uncle George is convinced that Louis should be treated at Davos. He says that modern opinion is in favour of mountain air for consumptives.'

I had an uncomfortable feeling that she was stressing unduly the words 'modern opinion', but perhaps I was mistaken. In any event, it is my belief that no one should be described as 'consumptive', a word which in effect defines a person in terms of a disease. I myself was labelled as a 'consumptive' when I was a Royal Navy surgeon, and for all I know the word is still there on my service record. At that time, so many years ago, 'modern opinion' favoured Madeira as the place for a 'cure', and I took seven months leave on half-pay to visit the island; admittedly, this was as much for the sake of my wife's health as my own, but it seemed to help. Nowadays, the climate of Madeira is regarded as too moist.

'You are correct, Mrs. Stevenson, in saying that modern opinion favours the mountain climate for patients with tuberculosis.'

Correct indeed. The Germans and Swiss had been at the forefront of this development during the previous twenty years or so, and their ideas had gradually gained acceptance. As a matter of fact, though, it was an Englishman called George Bodington who was the first to advocate the benefits of fresh air. It's a curious fact, certainly interesting to me, that the discovery resulted from Bodington's heavy workload. He had an extensive and widely scattered practice near Birmingham, and it was this that enabled him to see what had been hidden from others: country people are less prone to consumption than city dwellers. Bodington wrote up his observations in the form of a monograph, arguing against the prevailing view, the 'modern opinion' of that time you might say, which maintained that cold air had a bad influence on the disease. That was back in 1840, but the review of the monograph in *The Lancet* was so sarcastic, so patronising, that he gave up his practice and became proprietor of an asylum. Many years passed before his work was rediscovered. His conclusions became accepted only after the Army Sanitary Commission found that the high death rate from tuberculosis of the lungs in soldiers was related to overcrowding and poor ventilation.

I explained all this to the Stevensons. Louis, whose gaze had wandered over my shoulder to the window, to the other side of Cavendish Square and probably beyond that, slowly turned his face back towards me. 'As you say, doctor. As you say.'

I was beginning to enjoy myself. I stood up and walked to and fro, in imitation of myself as a teacher, not to mimic Louis.

The pitch of my voice rose, as if I was addressing a large group of students.

'It was a German doctor called Hermann Brehmer who set up the first mountain sanatorium, about 25 years ago. This was at Göbersdorf: fresh mountain air and good diet! Certainly he claimed excellent results, and others soon followed his example. Davos, with its long hours of sunshine during the winter months, is now well established as a health resort. No one can deny that.'

As I was speaking, I pulled a volume out of the bookshelves. Nearly a stone in weight, bound in calfskin, embossed with gold lettering on its four inch wide spine, three years old but still retaining the luscious smell of new leather: *The Lancet* for 1877. I carried the tome to my desk and turned the pages to a well-thumbed article.

'It's a report on a visit to Davos by Dr. Allbutt, a physician from The General Infirmary at Leeds.'

I did not mention that it was in this very article that Allbutt had accused me of 'serving old wine in old bottles'. I have my own way of facing up to criticism, and I will not allow gratuitous insults to cloud my judgement of a medical paper.

'Apparently, consumption is unknown among people who have always lived at Davos, presumably because of the purity of the air at more than five thousand feet above sea level. The snowtime is November to April, usually with four or five hours of sunshine a day during the season. His report on the medical regime is favourable, with no sign of any 'machinery of quackery', as he puts it.'

As I was speaking, Fanny's face relaxed into a softer, more respectful expression. It was clear that, for her, the words of *The*

Lancet carried weight. I have never understood why the process of printing should confer a level of authority denied to the verbal opinion; some of us choose to rely on the power of the spoken word to impress others with our beliefs, and we do have all the variations of pitch and volume, the sheer physicality of speech, at our disposal. In my experience, physicians who write learned articles for *The Lancet* do not necessarily possess that most basic, but sometimes most elusive, of medical skills, namely the ability to recognise whether or not a patient is actually ill. Not surprisingly, my own contributions to medical literature could be (and have been) described as insignificant.

'Thank you for giving us those words.' The reverential tone of Fanny's voice would have been more appropriate in a biblical context. And yet I have to confess that I was gratified to gain a sign of her approval, even though I had used *The Lancet* to achieve this. 'You've confirmed what Uncle George told us,' she continued. 'It really does give us a chance to cure Louis. So can we take it that you approve of our plan to spend the winter in Davos?'

How could I disagree? In reality, the plans had already been made, and my job was to confirm the wisdom of Dr. George Balfour's advice. Although I thought it unlikely that Louis had consumption, I couldn't rule out the diagnosis: only time would tell. In any case, the climate at Davos would no doubt have a beneficial effect on bronchiectasis, and surely no harm could result from a few months' stay at the resort. There was just the uneasy feeling that anyone sent to a centre specialising in the treatment of consumption would be regarded as suffering from the disease, whether or not this was the case, and a proposed stay of 'a few months' might insidiously be extended to the much quoted 'two winters and a summer needed for a complete cure'. After all, the financial well-being of a resort such as Davos must depend on the number of patients recruited, and on their length of stay. I still retain my innate distrust of specialism, my conviction that doctors treating only one disease will always have a vested interest in exaggerating its importance; ambition for self advance is, after all, part of human nature, especially in professional people. In talking to Louis, however, it would not have been helpful for me to express any doubt about a decision which I was expected to endorse.

'Yes, of course I approve of your plan to go to Davos, and you are going at exactly the right time of year, with the winter season ahead of you. To make good progress, remember always to follow the advice of your physician in Davos. And what an opportunity to write books! Use your time in the mountains well, Louis, and we will all be the richer for it.'

And so with these words I produced the required opinion. At the same time, I reflected that, if climatic treatment really did prove to be of great benefit to sufferers from consumption, then this was not going to be of any help to my East End patients, effectively imprisoned in the impure atmosphere of Whitechapel; for them, awareness of the diagnosis meant, quite simply, the destruction of all hope.

After Louis and Fanny had left Cavendish Square, I made a few more notes. Realisation crystallized in my mind. Louis and Fanny had talked to me and they had talked to each other, but they hadn't really listened to me. Each of them, independently, had picked at my words, choosing only a few morsels to nourish a particular point of view. I couldn't expect to achieve more than this. Sometimes, practicality represents a version of the truth. And, however you might define the truth of this matter, I believe that I played a part which enabled Louis Stevenson to fulfil his destiny.

Part Two:
Dr. Karl Ruedi's Narrative

Chapter Eight

THE WINTER OF 1880. The snow came late to the Davos valley that year, the year that I first met him. It was the third week in November before the ground was covered with its seasonal white blanket. The Stevensons had arrived earlier that month, ending their four week voyage with a seven hour stagecoach ride from the rail terminus at Landquart to the village of Davos-Platz. A wheeled coach, not the winter sleigh normally in use at that time of the year. And it brought them to an atmosphere of mist and gloom, the very opposite of our much-advertised Alpine picture of bright sunshine and blue sky.

After the mist had cleared and the snow had come, however, surely they must have seen the beauty of the valley. Whiteness startling in its extent and brightness, broken only by the banks of pine trees bordering the village. Mountains ranging up another five thousand feet, dominating the valley on three sides, protecting it from the cold north wind and trapping in the comforting heat of the sun's rays. And, nestling in the north west side of the valley, the village itself: only a few dozen buildings, but invested with a most dignified appearance by the elegantly tall, thin spire of its church.

The Stevensons were guests at the Belvedere, our most attractive and popular hotel, which had been opened some five years earlier by J.C. Coester, a proprietor who was without doubt an astute businessman, catering predominantly for British guests. The Belvedere had already established a reputation for efficiency, its timetable being run with railroad precision, but even then it was an expensive hotel, its bills inflated by various 'extras'. It was as modern as the geography and structure of Davos-Platz in 1880 would allow. In those days we had no drainage system in the village; the cesspools were cleared out each spring to manure the grass, creating a foul stench, which cleared only gradually as the soil absorbed the sewage.

By mid-December of that year the valley was deep in snow, and brilliant with sunshine for four or five hours each day, so that there was a feeling of warmth even when the temperature was below freezing point. The 'season' was well under way, with the village populated mainly by invalids. But these were invalids who appeared superficially well, their bronzed faces glossing over their bodily disease. And they were invalids who knew the nature of each other's sickness as well as their own, for the obvious reason that they were staying at a health resort for the treatment of one disease and one disease only: consumption.

Consumption had become the lifeblood of Davos. Even some of the tradespeople were consumptive, including our bookseller, Herr Richter, who had come to the village fifteen years earlier together with his friend Dr. Unger, a fellow sufferer, a medical man now generally regarded as the first to promote the region as a health resort. By 1880 Davos boasted eight other physicians, all experienced in the treatment of consumption, and all grateful to Dr. Unger for the success of his publicity.

At that time I, Karl Ruedi, one of these physicians, looked after most of the British patients. It was natural for me to do so. I was born less than 40 miles from Davos but, soon after graduating in medicine, I emigrated from my native land to Colorado. It was there that I learnt to speak fluent English. In due course I came back to Switzerland and settled in Davos as the District Doctor. Within four years of my return, and by now married to an Englishwoman, I had built up a good enough reputation to resign from officialdom and set up in private practice, catering to the increasing number of British guests at the health resort. My specialty is lung disease or, in other words, consumption.

I will tell you about a morning in December, a morning when the sun shone brightly, with a light both intense and dazzling reflected off a fresh covering of snow on the ground. I stood on the balcony of the Stevensons' room at the Belvedere, leaning on the rail next to Fanny, looking out for the return of Louis from his morning walk. The air was still, its quietness punctuated only by occasional, distant shouting: sounds of extraordinary clarity, and yet of no decipherable meaning.

We stood, we waited, we gazed. Fanny, impatient and uncomfortable, was apologetic. 'He promised that he'd be back by 11 o'clock, but he took my son Lloyd with him, and of course a 12-year-old boy needs more exercise than a 30-year-old invalid. They've probably taken one of the longer walks.' Not that there was much choice, she might have added; the number of walks was limited by the number of paths cut out of the snow, and it was not only Louis who complained of the tedious sameness of those white tracks.

'I'm disappointed that he isn't following more carefully the timetable that I recommended to him,' I replied. 'You can't separate treatment from the pattern of daily living, and in Davos that must always be under medical direction.' I was aware that my tall stature and booming voice lent to my words an authority which might have sounded harsh, but my manner was genial enough.

'Well, doctor, he's out of bed by half past six in the morning, and he always, always drinks at least four glasses of milk a day, but his appetite may not be good enough for him to eat every course of every meal.'

I turned to face her. I loosed a groan of disapproval. 'Adequate nutrition is part of the treatment, and sometimes an unwilling patient may require persuasion to eat his meals. I can't promise a cure if he doesn't follow the regimen. In any case, it's obvious that he needs to gain weight – unlike your good self, dear lady.'

She laughed loudly at the directness of my remark, perhaps resenting it. No one could deny that she was stout, although you might say that a 40-year-old mother of three should be expected to have such a figure. Like so many overweight ladies of her age, she could move with remarkable agility, and she could work faster than many a slim contemporary. On first meeting her, I had advised a reducing diet without bothering to ask if she wished to be one of my patients; subsequently, her weight had increased, although only by a few pounds.

'I'll try to curb my habit of eating bread between meals, doctor, but I do need something to comfort me at times. I'm not a lung invalid myself and this altitude doesn't really suit me. Hardly a day goes by without a dizzy spell or a palpitation. My head aches continuously and, when I say continuously, I mean day and night.'

I said nothing, preferring to keep private my view that her headaches were not likely to be related to the altitude as such. Davos is only about five thousand feet above sea level, and the Stevensons had travelled up at a leisurely pace; in any case, they had arrived several weeks earlier, and Fanny's symptoms were of more recent origin. The wives and husbands of the Davos invalids have their own problems, and it is not surprising that their bodies sometimes show signs of rebellion against their captive status.

'I can't really complain,' continued Fanny, 'because I know that we can cure Louis's consumption here in Davos, with your help of course Dr. Ruedi. I'm married to a brilliant writer, a man of genius, and therefore my own illnesses are of secondary importance. I want you to understand that I accept that.'

I nodded in acquiescence, out of courtesy rather than actual agreement. I knew that Louis was a writer, but at that time he was a writer who was almost unknown, even in his own country. Of the other British guests and residents, only John Addington Symonds, an established critic and historian, had recognised Louis's name prior to the Stevensons' arrival in Davos, and even Symonds hadn't been able to tell me much about him. I was aware that Louis's income came from his father and not from his publications; this much had been made clear in a letter from Dr. George Balfour, who had written to me with medical details and background information, including a few of his own suggestions for treatment. As far as payment of medical bills was concerned, Louis's position was sound, and there was no reason for me to concern myself with the merits or commercial value of his literary work.

'Here's Louis now.' Fanny pointed to the narrow figure trudging along the path at the front of the hotel, his shoulders hunched forwards and his hands deep in his coat pockets. Just behind him was his stepson, zigzagging across the path and its borders, with unrestrained joyous energy. I wondered why Lloyd wasn't attending lessons with the tutor that the Stevensons had hired from among the Davos residents, but it was not my job to question the domestic arrangements of my patients and their families.

Fanny half smiled, and shrugged. 'Lloyd worships Louis. They spend hours together, playing with hundreds of lead soldiers: quite serious games, I assure you, involving complicated military tactics. Louis has been studying a big book called *Operations of War* and Lloyd has been writing up war correspondence. At present, I don't feel brave enough to tell Louis that he should be doing some writing himself, but I do worry about his lack of energy.'

'Remember that I have ordered him to restrict his writing to two hours each morning for the time being,' I replied. 'He needs mental rest as well as bodily exercise. It's all part of the treatment.'

We retreated from the balcony to the room as the door was flung open and the pair clattered in, stamping their feet and powdering the air with snow as they pulled off their coats.

'Louis, Louis,' shouted Lloyd, ignoring both Fanny and myself, 'let's get on with the battle.'

'Later, I think.' His manner was more that of an elder brother than a stepfather. 'I've some even more serious business to attend to first. Leave us with the doctor for half an hour, old chap.'

Louis slipped off his jacket, flannel shirt and thick woollen vest so that I could examine him. He stood with his arms hanging down limply as I tapped at his chest with my fingers and listened systematically to the breath sounds with a stethoscope. As a rule, I ask my patients to stand for examination, simply because my outlook is effectively limited to the chest, my area of expertise. I wish to be regarded as a lung specialist, and I particularly discourage discussion of symptoms affecting any part of the body below the diaphragm, usually replying to attempts at such conversation with the words: 'Sir (or Madam), please remember that I am a doctor of the lung'.

After Louis had put his shirt back on and was seated, I took a thermometer out of its leather case, carefully inspected it and then vigorously shook down the mercury column before placing the bulb under his tongue.

'Now we'll leave that there for seven minutes,' I told him, checking the time on my pocket watch. Seven minutes may be excessive, but this is my practice, and it does give me the opportunity to speak at some length without interruption by the patient.

'I do believe that the disease is static.' I suppose that this statement somehow carried the assumption that the disease in question was consumption; if I had ever entertained any doubt about the diagnosis, then I had put this to the back of my mind, believing that any debate on the subject would lead to uncertainty and confusion.

'Of course, to achieve lasting arrest of the disease process, we generally need two winters and a summer. Recovery is a slow process. The cold air has an 'anti-phlogistic' or anti-inflammatory effect on the lungs, but this isn't immediate: it depends on time, and the beneficial effect of low atmospheric pressure in increasing the expansion of the chest and lungs. You must give the mountain air, with its wonderful purity and high ozone content, plenty of time to exert its beneficial effect.'

'Can Louis do anything more to help himself, doctor?' asked Fanny.

'Follow the regimen and timetable closely, please Mr. Stevenson. Take a cold bath each morning. Eat all your meals and most especially the fat: it produces heat. Drink four litres of milk a day. Take your cod-liver oil in a glass of Marsala after lunch. Drink at least two thirds of a litre of our Veltliner wine every single day, to stimulate the heart. Take all your walks methodically, breathing through your nose and avoiding any talk. There are so many ways in which you can help yourself, if you're prepared to follow medical instructions.'

As always, I tried to inject concerned friendliness into my pronouncements, which otherwise might have sounded dogmatic. I have a strong belief in the importance of strict and precise regimens; there is no doubt about this in my mind. Of course, at that time I felt frustrated by the free and easy atmosphere in the hotels. My dearest wish was for the development of a sanatorium at Davos, a sanatorium that would allow proper control and medical supervision of patients; clearly, this would benefit all concerned, and would eliminate the 'holiday' ambience of the hotels. I dreamt of a sanatorium which would be a fitting memorial to my father, Luzius Ruedi, the very first medical man to open a practice in Davos, the man who should have been credited with discovering the beneficial effects of our climate; as long ago as 1841, he had opened an institution for the treatment of consumptive children, only for it to close all too soon as financial support was withdrawn. How quickly were the ties of friendship loosened when profits failed to materialise! The good name of Davos as a health resort is now associated with the 'pioneering' work of Unger and Spengler, but it was Luzius Ruedi who was the true pioneer. And in 1880, when I was about the same age as my father had been in 1841, I felt a powerful, disturbing sense of identity with him, and at the same time a sense of foreboding that my own career would come to a similar, ignominious end.

I pulled the thermometer out of Louis's mouth and slowly rolled the instrument in front of my eyes to locate the mercury column, hiding in there and then suddenly appearing, glistening, revealing in that moment the state of the disease. I made a note of the temperature reading. Just a single reading. I would have preferred a record of the temperatures at least four times a day; in a sanatorium I would have been able to train my patients to take their own readings, but I could hardly expect hotel guests to undertake such a task.

'98·4 degrees on the Fahrenheit scale, Mr. Stevenson: precisely normal, I'm glad to say. It's likely that you have some infiltration of the lungs, probably chronic pneumonia and certainly a bronchitic tendency, but I do believe that the disease has come to a halt. There can be no doubt that you're benefiting from our treatment at Davos, and I recommend that you now take more exercise each day.'

Fanny, shaking a little, apparently attempting to control a snigger, turned to look through the window and stared intently at the horizon. I realized that, not unusually for me, I had given a robust medical opinion without asking the patient how he felt. I doubt that this would have amused her, however; it was more likely that she had found something comical in the Colorado influence on my accent.

Louis looked sideways in her direction for less than a second, just long enough to transmit an invisible wave of rapport through the ether. 'I'm relieved to hear what you say, doctor. Exercise is a fine thing, of course, but I think you'll agree with me when I say that walking in Davos is somewhat restricted, in variety if not in distance. Every walk's the same: snow as far as the eye can see. It hides all the colour of the landscape and masks every scent, except for the smell of frost. In any case, there's no scope for the solitary walker, for the writer who needs to think; every path has its line of invalids. It reminds me all the time of my own state of decay.'

'Come now, Mr. Stevenson, surely the space and the wonderful air give you a sense of freedom.'

'No, no. On the contrary, I feel caged in by the mountains. The air is good and pure, I grant you, but it seems to endow me with a curious acceptance of things, a languor that I can't overcome. I no longer worry that the two hours a day allowed for work seems too much. I'm a writer who can't write, although I'm quite good at sitting with a piece of paper in front of me.'

Louis was slumped in his chair, rubbing his forehead with the long, boney fingers of his right hand. His eyes, half hidden, peered out at me through the gaps between his fingers.

'What I'm trying to say, Dr. Ruedi, is that my lungs may be doing well, but I am not.'

'If your lungs are doing well, what more can we ask at present?' Fanny threw the words at him. 'You haven't had a single cold since you came here, and colds have always been your enemy. The writing can come later, Louis, and in the meantime we must find other diversions for you.'

'My dear fellow,' replied Louis, addressing Fanny in a manner that I found puzzling, 'there's a limit to the appeal of billiards, cards, draughts and dominoes. And there's a limit to the appeal of our fellow guests in the hotel.'

'Louis, it's obvious that you enjoy talking for hours and

hours to Symonds. I'm glad of that for your sake, however condescending his attitude to me may be.'

'His attitude is condescending to me as well,' admitted
Louis, sniffing. 'He never fails to remind me that my knowledge
of literature is self-taught, and lacking in the nice discipline of a
Balliol education. Yes, I enjoy talking to him and listening to
him, but I doubt that our friendship will extend beyond our time
together here in Davos.'

I remained silent. Symonds was a patient of mine, and therefore I could not enter into any discussion about him, although I
might have an opinion. An Englishman of precise manners who,
being the son of a physician, had an overt disrespect for the medical profession but at the same time more than a streak of depen-
dence on his doctors. A married man with four daughters. A
man who was attracted to the young males of the neighbourhood. Paradoxically, Louis, who shone and revelled in the company of men, may not have been aware of his friend's proclivi-
ties; sometimes naivety goes hand in hand with creativity. It was
not a subject suitable for conversation.

'Have you tried tobogganing, Mr. Stevenson?'

'Yes, indeed, dear doctor. That's something I really do enjoy,
and I say that with truthfulness. Sitting on a toboggan, speeding
downhill and using your feet to steer is an exhilarating experience, and most exhilarating of all at night, alone under the stars
in 40 degrees of frost. You can keep your skating and let me
have my tobogganing.'

I frowned. 'Mr. Stevenson, I don't think that tobogganing at
night is necessarily to be recommended. I strongly suggest
restricting the pastime to mid-afternoon.'

With this attempt to instil a sense of order into Louis's daily life at the resort, I prepared to take my leave. Unfortunately, this proved to be a leave-taking lacking in dignity, interrupted as it was by the re-entrance of Lloyd, not alone but accompanied by a growling, yapping mass of long black hair on four short legs.

'Woggs, Woggs, come here you naughty dog,' shouted Lloyd with confident authority. 'Don't worry, doctor, he won't do any harm. He's just being silly.'

With this, the Stevensons' Skye terrier sank its teeth into my right ankle, producing a human yelp almost as impressive as its own. To this day, I can still push my fingers down inside my sock and feel the scars of the attack, an attack imprinted on my memory as well as on my ankle, and yet no doubt forgotten by those who observed it.

Fanny disengaged the beast. 'It's nothing personal. He's bitten me more than once. I put it down to his epilepsy: he has quite violent fits at times, and then lies unconscious for hours.'

'Perhaps some reduction in his level of consciousness would be helpful,' I replied, in a tone of voice which was remarkably restrained, considering the anger that I felt swirling inside me. 'As you know, we discourage medication here, but in the case of your dog, I'll make an exception and prescribe a daily dose of bromide.'

Soon afterwards, I was able to make my escape from the hotel. It was going to be hard work to persuade the Stevensons to stay in Davos for eighteen months, and I was beginning to feel that failure might be preferable to success.

Chapter Nine

BY EARLY APRIL OF 1881, five months after the Stevensons' arrival in Davos, I had accepted that they would 'go down' from the mountain resort, at least for the summer season. I could no longer evade the question 'How long must I stay here?': the question heard so often in Davos, the question to which there could never be a satisfactory answer. After weeks of discussion, I acquiesced in their plan to return to Scotland, on condition that they journeyed to the Highlands via the Glasgow route. As a matter of fact, I know next to nothing about the geography of Scotland. It was Fanny, fearing that Louis would become exhausted if he entertained his friends in Edinburgh, who persuaded me to translate her opinion into my medical 'advice', despite knowing that Louis would ignore this when he escaped from Davos. The words of a doctor can provide useful ammunition in the battle between husband and wife.

It was a difficult time for all of us. The first few days in April were dominated by the death of Bertie, the 18-year-old son of Louis's friend Mrs. Sitwell. The boy and his mother had arrived in Davos some three months earlier, but unfortunately the disease was too far advanced for there to be any realistic chance of a cure; this was a case of 'galloping' consumption which lived up to its name. From the first moment that I saw Bertie I knew that he was dying and that there was no treatment, no intervention, no miracle that could change the course of events so clearly mapped out in front of him. And yet, in a case such as this, a doctor must be all the more diligent; the value of his advice is derived, not from any knowledge of illness or remedies, but from his acquaintanceship with death.

I must emphasise that prospective patients should travel to the resort early in the course of the disease. The physicians of Davos are willing to treat all comers, of course, but there is no doubt that deaths, however discreetly managed, discourage the other patients, as well as distorting the statistics which are needed to advertise the important benefits of the mountain air.

Soon after her arrival in Davos, Fanny had acquainted me with the harrowing details of the death from consumption of her son Hervey, and therefore I was not surprised that her symptoms worsened as she witnessed Bertie's decline. The aching at the front of her head became heavier by the day; she felt as though an iron band was being tightened round her skull, squeezing her brain and stopping all thought other than that of the pain itself. Whenever she sat still, she could feel her heart pounding, demanding respite for her tortured mind and body. What was it that was happening to her? What was the cause of her anguish? She blamed the altitude, but she was prepared to suffer it for Louis's sake. Anger was her reaction to any suggestion of under-lying nervousness, and so I had to seek refuge behind my lung specialist's status, advising her to take a week's trip to Paris for consultation with doctors more eminent than myself. Telegrams and letters explaining her medical history were sent ahead of her. Detailed plans were made for her journey. Complex arrange-ments were put in place for appropriate expenditure on the trip. All of this activity was in itself therapeutic, diverting her atten-tion away from me, her regular medical adviser, the man who stood too close to be believed. In this way, I was able to get Fanny out of Davos during the most distressing stages of Bertie's illness. As events turned out, she arrived back the day before his death, but the escape to Paris undoubtedly spared her much of the wretchedness felt by those who witnessed the last week on earth of that brave boy.

It was on the day after Bertie's death that I called at the Belvedere to see the Stevensons, knowing that this would be for the last time before they left Davos on their journey back to Scotland.

'Mr. Stevenson, it's been a privilege to look after you during the last few months. Can we agree that your stay in Davos has been beneficial to you?'

'Perhaps so, compared to some others. How do you explain a disease that carries off a strong young man like Bertie and leaves a frail stick like myself still standing? I suppose that I should feel grateful. Certainly I must thank you for your kindness to Bertie and Mrs. Sitwell.'

I acknowledged the compliment with a modest inclination of my head. It is true that, when faced with a young person on the decline, my domineering manner becomes subdued by the awesome nature of death. And when all can see that the fight is lost and the end near, I marvel at the comfort and beauty of that period of acceptance, the transition from trivial concerns to a more profound level of thought. It is at such times that I reach back to my true, childlike, personality, undisguised by the robust bluffness that has become my second nature.

Fanny, bright and businesslike, no longer with furrowed brow and downcast look, eyed me directly. 'Incidentally, we'd be grateful if you could persuade Herr Coester not to add too many extras to Mrs. Sitwell's bill. We've heard rumours that he's likely to charge her not only for Bertie's mattress and bedclothes, but also for the bedstead.'

'Oh no, that's not true,' I replied. 'He'll charge for the bedding, which then becomes the property of whoever's paid for it, and they are at liberty to donate it to the poor of the village. After all, you can't expect hotel guests to sleep on bedding in which former patients have died. I promise you that he never charges for the bedstead: that would be profiteering.'

There was a pause before Louis returned to the original question. 'As far as my health's concerned, I have to say that I've lost weight since Christmas, despite all your tonics, cod-liver oil, wines and beef tea. I had a heavy cold in January, even though colds are not supposed to exist in Davos, where we're so much higher up than your famous 'immunity line' of three thousand feet above sea level. And then came horrible bronchitis. A few days ago, to cap it all, I coughed up, not the usual yellow stuff, but something worse: blood. I felt as if the whole of my winter's imprisonment here had been in vain when I saw that vile red blotch slowly expanding in the snow, as if my life blood was being sucked into those sterile crystals. I'm not a mercenary type: otherwise, I should ask what we've been paying for here during the last few months. The fact is that my health is no better, and my spirits are low. I haven't written anything worthwhile since I arrived in Davos, and perhaps I never will. Yesterday, I overheard one of the other hotel guests talking about me: 'Stevenson? Oh yes – hasn't he written something or other?' That, Dr. Ruedi, could well be my epitaph.'

'Courage, Mr. Stevenson,' I replied. 'Remember that it's early days. We need another year at least, perhaps longer. With this disease, a cure cannot be hurried.'

Fanny leaned forward in her chair and looked intently at Louis. It seemed to me that, despite her various nervous complaints, she radiated determination and strength of character. The amber skin of her face, darkened by the winter's sunshine, contrasted sharply with the whites of her wide open eyes and with her shiny, perfect teeth. There was a firm set to her jaw, and a wilfulness about her mouth, as she spoke.

'Now see here, Louis, we haven't spent the last five months in Davos just so that you can give up the ghost. This altitude's attacked my health like the devil, but it'll be worth it in the long run if you get better. All the doctors have agreed that your lungs need to be in the mountains, and so that's where you must be. There's no alternative if we're going to cure the disease and get you back writing again.'

Louis grimaced: a grimace of thinly disguised pleasure. 'It appears that Fanny is going to deprive me of the pleasure of fading away. I suppose that means that I must continue the struggle. And then, who knows? Maybe, just maybe, I will regain enough strength to make proper use of my pen and ink again.'

'I can promise you that another winter in Davos would definitely benefit you, and would lead to a permanent arrest of the disease process,' I replied. 'I recommend renting a chalet for the next season: I think we all agree that hotel life doesn't suit you.'

'It certainly doesn't suit my pocket. I've already had to send to my father for another hundred pounds to cover the cost of Coester's wine bills and tobogganing fees. You can be sure that nothing would induce me to stay at the Belvedere again.'

I gave a neutral smile. Whatever Louis might say, it was clear that Fanny would bring him back to the resort at the beginning of the next winter. For good or ill, Davos would be given another opportunity.

Chapter Ten

THE NEXT WINTER WAS unusually mild for Davos. There was snow, but it was not the thick covering which residents and visitors expect as a matter of course. It seemed more like springtime, with green grass appearing before our eyes to break the continuity of the white carpet. By the middle of February 1882, sleigh traffic had become impracticable and the daily post arrived by a wheeled coach that was normally stored away in the early months of the year.

I was not in a good temper. The arrival of the Föhn, moaning and whistling among the buildings of the village, had pushed up the temperature of the valley by several degrees within a matter of hours. Even natives of the area, such as myself, are vulnerable to the depressing qualities of the warm south wind, with its peculiar capacity to provoke vague, unfathomable feelings of guilt. Unlike my patients, I was not in a position to close up the shutters and stay indoors until the wind had subsided; I had to continue my rounds, demonstrating each day my indispensability. It was at times such as this that I hankered after my old job as District Physician, paid a salary every month, regardless of work done or not done. As a private practitioner, my rewards were greater, but dependent on, and proportional to, the number of patients actually seen and satisfied. That is something different. I couldn't afford to take time off simply because I felt unwell; my patients would no doubt genuinely regret my absence but would not delay long before calling out one of my colleagues, who would unsettle them by questioning or even contradicting my advice. In those days, competition among the doctors of Davos was such that agreement between two of them was unusual, and between more than two of them unknown.

It was already dark by the time that I arrived, tired and irritable, at the Stevensons' chalet. The Chalet am Stein, so called because of its proximity to a great stone, was higher up than the Belvedere, and well separated from it. It was a generously sized chalet, sometimes known as a villa for this reason, with an extensive balcony and overhanging roof. The main room was half-lit by a single oil-lamp as I banged on the door and walked straight in uninvited, with the easy familiarity that is generally conceded to a regular medical attendant.

Fanny greeted me with a warmth which, I regret to say, was undeserved. During the previous two or three months, the state of her health had been even worse than that of Louis. I now admit that my diagnostic ability failed at every stage, although I can console myself with the knowledge that she was not a lung patient, not really a Davos patient at all. After weeks of delay, during which she was suffering with frequent attacks of griping abdominal pain and swelling, I had sent her to Berne for further medical advice. The eminent specialist there got it spectacularly wrong as well, diagnosing ulceration of the bowel, probably malignant, possibly fatal. It was only after she had actually passed a gallstone and recovered from the acute attack that we finally realised she had nothing more or less than gall-bladder disease, which in truth was the first diagnosis we should have considered. By that stage, I had dispatched Louis, who was desperately worried that he was going to lose her, to Berne. They returned a few days later, miserably cold, after a seven hour ride from Landquart in an open sleigh, and perhaps they were lucky to hire any sort of sleigh: it was Christmas Day. Yes, I now acknowledge that my incompetence endangered the lives of both Fanny and Louis. Paradoxically, the Stevensons' faith in my professional ability was, if anything, strengthened by these events; I was as welcome as ever at the Chalet am Stein.

Welcome, that is, except in the eyes of Woggs who, identifying me as an enemy, circled and yapped around my feet.

'Quiet, Woggs!' Fanny's order had no discernible effect on the dog's frenzied activity. 'Quiet, quiet, quiet,' she repeated, holding her hands to her ears.

'That canker of his ear is giving him the devil of a pain, doctor. He doesn't seem to realise that you've been helping him by supplying laudanum. It's as good for him as it is for me.'

'Perhaps he's due for another dose. I doubt that Mr. Stevenson will be able to work with that noise in the background,' I replied, although it did seem to me that Louis, despite complaining about the incessant barking of dogs in Davos, would tolerate any behaviour that Woggs cared to indulge in.

'Oh, he's not working at the moment. He's up in the attic with Lloyd, fighting the battle of Waterloo. My son has given him the opportunity to relive his childhood, and how he's enjoying that! Secretly, he loves nothing more than being confined to his quarters.'

Louis had developed a painful knee, which effectively restricted him to the chalet. In normal circumstances, I would have adopted a policy of 'wait and see', but in this case I had immediately put in a request for a surgeon to visit and advise them. If anything further was to go wrong, I wanted them to say 'at least Dr. Ruedi realised that it was sufficiently serious to require an urgent second opinion, and it wasn't his fault that the surgeon botched it up'. In the meantime, any pretence that Louis was following a regime of treatment for his lung disease had been quietly dropped. Exercise was impracticable, and the diet at Chalet am Stein was unpredictable. As for the daily quota of alcohol, the number of empty Veltliner bottles at the door suggested that this exceeded medical recommendations by a wide margin.

At Fanny's invitation, I climbed up the ladder to the attic and peered in at an extraordinary sight. The whole area of the floor was chalked as a battleground: roads, rivers, fields and hills all separately, meticulously, coloured. Hundreds of lead soldiers were deployed in their units, cavalry as well as infantry; miniature tents with paper flags represented the various headquarters. On the floorboards of the attic, at the boundaries of the battleground, there were five or six candles, illuminating the armies, and casting on to the slopes of the ceiling shadows of all shapes and sizes, shuddering briefly in the draught generated by my entrance. Louis and Lloyd were sitting on the floor at opposite ends of the room, with documents lined up in front of them.

'Come on up, Ruedi,' shouted Louis, 'I need your advice on a matter of tactics.'

'Have a look at these dispatches: they're printed on the Davos Press,' yelled Lloyd in his uninhibited high-pitched voice, with the natural, infectious excitement of a 13-year-old boy. He had made something of a name for himself with an amateur printing press, brought over from San Francisco, and had got himself appointed as the official printer of hotel concert programmes. In addition (and he often boasted about this) he was the publisher of Robert Louis Stevenson's *A Martial Elegy on Some Lead Soldiers*.

I scrambled into the attic. Too tall to stand in the confined space, I squatted on the floor by the window which, ajar, overlooked the village, now all in darkness except for the scattered flickering of oil-lamps and candles.

'I've no military experience, Stevenson. I can only advise you on medical matters.'

Louis laughed in a good-natured way.

'Military matters and cartography are good for my health, and for my literary output. After all, it was a map drawn with Lloyd's help in Scotland last summer that set me off writing *Treasure Island*. And, my dear Ruedi, the serialisation of the tale in *Young Folks* has now been completed, making me richer by 34 pounds seven and six. Not bad, I think you'll agree, for a story written without any agonising over style or psychological content.'

Louis's publication of *Treasure Island* under the curious pseudonym of 'Captain George North' was puzzling to me. According to local gossip, it was not what had been expected of our literary patient. Later on, after Louis had left Davos, I read the story and realised that it was more than just a rattling good tale. Mark my words: the names of Jim Hawkins, Long John Silver and Ben Gunn will live on into the twentieth century.

'Not bad at all, Stevenson, and I think you'll agree that we in Davos can take some credit for it. It's well known in the village that you finished writing the story after you had returned here this winter. And good writing depends on good health.'

'That may be an accepted medical view but it doesn't fit in with my experience,' replied Louis. 'The fact of the matter is that I started writing the story last summer in Braemar, when my health was at a low ebb. The weather was foul, and I had a horrid cold, and then blood spitting again.

When my Uncle George came to visit us, he was so horrified by the state of my bellows that he made me wear a respirator, rather like a pig's snout, for inhaling pine-oil. And yet it was at Braemar that I got cracking with *Treasure Island*: 15 chapters, at a rate of a chapter a day! Every evening I sat by an oil-lamp in that tiny cottage and read aloud to anyone who cared to listen. Lloyd spurred me on. As for my father, he was enthusiasm personified; at last I was writing something that he could take a pride in, something that could involve him. Admittedly, true to form, I ground to a halt after writing 15 chapters but by then the story had been accepted for serialisation. That meant there was no choice: I had to finish writing the other 19 chapters when I returned here to Davos.'

'Well, all I can say is that you returned in a poor state of health. Still with a violent cough, still spitting up blood, still insisting on dosing yourself with a mixture of chloral and hashish at night: definitely not what I would recommend. And as for your pine-oil respirator, forgive me for pointing out that, if you'd stayed in Davos all summer, you would have had a pine-wood on your doorstep.'

'We have pine-woods in Scotland as well, Ruedi, and you know that I couldn't have stuck it out at Davos through the summer. It's only the presence here of your excellent self that induced us to return for another winter, and I can't honestly say that it's helped my health so far. I haven't been out of the chalet for weeks.'

'That's because of Mrs. Stevenson's slow recovery and because of your swollen knee. You'll find that your lungs will gradually improve now that you're settled back here in Davos. My measurements show that your chest expansion has increased during the last few weeks.' Then, as now, my assessment of lung disease would always include a series of figures recorded to demonstrate improvement in the movements of the chest during breathing; I use a special pair of calipers, and an instrument called a 'cyrtometer', designed to measure curves. Louis never showed any interest in these results; he seemed to be incapable of appreciating the magic of numbers, the magic that can clothe a dubious proposition with a coat of authenticity.

'I don't know about chest measurements, but I have to admit that I'm feeling more optimistic than I did last winter. I've certainly been more productive, finishing off *Treasure Island* and writing up *The Silverado Squatters*, all within a few months.'

'And I suppose I have to admit that, really, I can't relate your increased productivity to any improvement in your health: the time sequence doesn't fit,' I replied. It was a display of frankness which would have been unimaginable a year earlier.

'You speak the truth, and yet I must say that you've helped us in many ways, Ruedi. This chalet has been a home-from-home for us: untidy, chaotic even, but our own place, with no risk of getting caught in polite conversation with hotel guests, people who have nothing in common with each other except an illness and a roof. The only thing that I miss from the Belvedere is their supply of real honey.'

'And the billiards,' butted in Lloyd, who had been bursting to join in the conversation at the first sign of any deviation from adult talk. 'Louis loves a game of billiards, doctor, but he's the world's worst player. As for dominoes, I can beat him at that any time.'

'May be, General Osbourne, but you can't beat me on the field of battle. Superior military tactics will always carry the day. Continue your doomed attack if you dare!'

I left the military commanders to their battle plans. As I made my way home, I gradually realised that I was looking around me, not at my feet. My head and body seemed lighter in weight. Louis, by accident or design, had somehow made me feel valued as a doctor and as a friend, just at a point in time when criticism would have been justified.

By the beginning of April, the Stevensons were preparing to leave Davos and I had to accept that this time they would not return. I could understand Louis's sense of imprisonment in the mountains and indeed I shared some of that feeling in myself, despite being a native of the region. Each day, I would devote a few minutes, sometimes longer, to imagining myself back in Colorado as the young doctor with a future, the young doctor who hadn't yet retreated to the home of his childhood, apparently destined to repeat his father's mistakes. If only I could accumulate enough capital to ensure security for my family, then I would return to the New World. But would I be too old by then to start a new practice? It was a daily reverie which was at the same time both enjoyable and painful, and to which there could be no conclusion in the foreseeable future.

Fanny wanted to know the state of Louis's lungs.

'Is it better or worse, doctor?'

'Certainly better than when he came back at the beginning of the winter. The signs of disease have receded: only a bit of nibbling now, compared with two thirds of a lung affected a year ago.'

'Only a bit of nibbling? You mean that there are fewer signs of consumption?'

'Yes, fewer signs of disease,' I replied, with caution. I knew about Dr. Andrew Clark's suggestion that Louis might have bronchiectasis rather than consumption, and I couldn't deny to myself that this was possible, or even probable. I also knew that agonising over the diagnosis would not be of any help to Louis at this stage. My conscience was clear: the climate of Davos had, in the end, led to an improvement in the state of Louis's lungs, and that was enough to justify everything. Louis himself was vague about medical matters and only interested in detail when it was of immediate importance; it was Fanny who was the 'doctor' in the family and if she was convinced that Louis had consumption, then it was not for me to express any doubts about this, especially in Davos. Why quarrel with our bread and butter?

'I can't thank you enough. You've been so kind to us. Davos hasn't been good for my health; I still need morphine and brandy some nights, but that's not important. Louis, despite his periods of illness, despite frequent interruptions by Lloyd, despite the barking of the village dogs, despite everything, has been working, and that's what matters.'

I nodded, curtly perhaps, but anything more would have been uncomfortably demonstrative. 'Long may it continue. Rest assured that he's well enough to leave Davos for a softer climate. I recommend the South of France, 15 miles as the crow flies from the sea, and near a pine-wood –'

My voice tailed off. Perhaps this was not an occasion for dogmatism. I had learnt something from Robert Louis Stevenson.

Part Three:
Dr. Thomas Bodley Scott's Narrative

Chapter Eleven

IT WAS AN EASY WALK down from my house on the Poole Road
to the Stevenson residence at the head of Alum Chine, which, for
those of you who don't know Bournemouth, is the most attractive of the deep, narrow ravines which cut through the cliffs
down to the sea. On that day in 1885 – a lovely autumn morning – I was as happy as can be, marching briskly down to
'Skerryvore' to see my favourite patient. Swinging my medical
bag, and whistling softly to myself, I thanked my maker for
granting me the privilege of living and working in such a delightful seaside town. The sun cut a bright yellow circle through the
thin haze, casting soft shadows of trees and houses on to the
roadway. A gentle sea breeze was blowing up through the pine-
trees of the chine: appetizing air of wonderful purity, every
breath cleansing the lungs. It is not in the least surprising that
the reputation of the town as a health resort continues to grow
year by year. Even in 1885, the population was well over
17,000, compared to nil at the beginning of the century. The
unique quality of our marvellous atmosphere depends on the
mixture of sea breeze, pine emanations and the drier air at the
top of the cliffs. The pine-trees represent a critical factor in this
equation, the curative property of pine in lung disease being
well-known, a matter of belief dating back to the ancient world.
This is why the local doctors are so disturbed at the tendency of
Bournemouth's men of property to dismiss the importance of the
conifers, preferring to clear areas for house building. Of course

this is understandable, in view of the ever-rising price of land in the region, but medical opinion is strongly opposed to pine clearing, which we regard as an act of short-sighted folly. The welfare of the town depends on its reputation as a health resort and this in turn depends on the special qualities of the Bournemouth air.

I would like to record something of my friendship with Robert Louis Stevenson. Before that, however, I must relate a little of my own history.

I settled in Bournemouth as a General Practitioner in 1876 and, since then, I have never regretted this decision for a single moment. Soon after my arrival, the local community generously and fully accepted me, not only as their doctor, but also as a Church Warden and, most important of all, as their friend. I love being the confidant of my patients, the man they can turn to at times of distress, the man who will always be willing to help them. Work is no burden to me, because so much of the job is enjoyable: the intimate conversations with my patients, the good relations with professional colleagues, the warm feeling of being needed. And yet, curiously, it was ill fortune that first brought me to Bournemouth. After my qualification as a doctor, my brief hospital career at St. Bartholomew's was brought to an end by an illness which forced me to leave the country and work for a year in the wholesome climate of Tasmania. It was Bournemouth's reputation as a health resort that attracted me after my return to England and marriage; Adeline insisted that my health and ease of mind should take priority over mercenary consider- ations. A wise decision! Although financial reward has never been the first priority, our income has grown nicely with the size of my practice and, coincidentally, with the size of our family.

More importantly, the role of General Practitioner suits my temperament; if I was made for anything, I was made for this.

What little I have told you about myself will be enough to explain why I felt so contented and so at peace with the world on that autumn day in 1885. A man in his right place; a man, moreover, in his mid-thirties, an age which for so many of us is the zenith of our lives, whether or not we recognise it as such at the time.

The entrance to Louis and Fanny's house on Alum Chine Road was marked by a model of Skerryvore, the Atlantic lighthouse that Thomas Stevenson had helped to build. Indeed the house itself was named 'Skerryvore', no doubt in recognition of Thomas's generosity in buying it for Fanny earlier that year. Built with the local yellow brick, partially covered with ivy, and roofed with blue slate, it stood out as an imposing detached villa, confident in style and typical of the area's housing. The side of the house away from the road overlooked the lawn and kitchen garden, with a path through the heather leading down among the pine-trees and rhododendron bushes to the bottom of the chine. Sometimes Louis was to be found seated down in the chine, reading or writing, but I knew that on this day he would be indoors, confined to the house by recent illness.

My approach to the house was, as usual, heralded by the clattering wings of the wood pigeons. These domesticated birds had remained resident in the garden despite the advent of Fanny's cat Ginger and the aggressive Stevenson Skye terrier called 'Bogue', a warrior previously known as 'Woggs'. The pigeons reacted to any perceived threat by flying up to the roof and perching there, sometimes for many hours, in rain or sun, secure in the knowledge that Fanny would eventually feed them, and that they would never have to fend for themselves.

I was shown into the dining room by Valentine, the maid who had accompanied the Stevensons from the south of France. It was Fanny and Lloyd who were there to welcome me, or perhaps waylay me before I could see Louis.

Fanny led me by the hand to a delicate Sheraton chair, on which I sat stiffly upright, resting my medical bag uncomfortably on my knees. I listened carefully to her words. 'He's still in bed, Dr. Scott. I don't think he's really recovered from that blood spitting he had in Exeter a few weeks ago, but of course I rely on your judgement.'

My judgement on this matter was by no means clear-cut. Ever since the Stevensons' move to Bournemouth the previous year, living at first in rented accommodation, Louis had been subject to repeated cough, influenza and fever. It was the blood spitting that alarmed Fanny. An ill-advised visit to the West Country had resulted in an episode serious enough to delay their return journey at Exeter's New London Hotel for several days. Fanny had reported back a 'dreadful haemorrhage', and I'd even volunteered to travel out to Devonshire if needed. Fortunately, Louis had returned home intact, but weakened.

Not for the first time, I was held by her steady gaze, a gaze of strength and trustworthiness. If I was asked now what she was wearing, my memory would fail me, save for an impression of careless dressing: the world would have to take her as she was.

Of course, I wanted her to know that I understood something of the anxiety that she felt about Louis's illness. My appearance – prematurely bald, avuncular beyond my years, and with a reassuring paunch – may in itself have been of some help. But I knew that she liked to hear the truth of the matter, and that nothing upset her more than humbug. 'Mrs. Stevenson, we have to face the fact that your husband has had several haemorrhages since he came to Bournemouth, and no doubt this tendency will continue. At the first sign of bleeding, you know what to do.'

'Oh yes, yes, the ergotine, of course. We've used that many times. It may be a good drug but it doesn't always work. Don't forget that I nursed Louis through a horrendous haemorrhage in the south of France last year. He was coughing blood every half hour, sometimes as much as a pint at a time, just *gushing* out. I tried everything: ergotine injections, mustard on his legs, an ice-bladder on his chest. It was only when he'd nearly fainted from loss of blood that the flow stopped. It must have been a burst artery I guess. I was so frightened that Louis's parents would hold me responsible if he died, and of course in the end I was blamed both for exaggeration and for not keeping them informed. Exaggeration! How could anyone know what happened in Hyères except Louis and myself? His cousin Bob and his friends Henley and Baxter sent out a doctor from London, but by the time this Dr. Mennell arrived the worst was over, and he made me feel that I'd overreacted like a hysterical female. He said it wasn't a ruptured vessel, patted me on the head and returned home, charging more than a hundred pounds for his services, which of course Louis's father had to pay for in the end. You'll forgive me, Dr. Scott, if my opinion of the medical profession is not as high as it might be.'

Fanny's eyes flashed with anger and righteous indignation. I was used to her outbursts, and I recognised the justification for them.

'Of course I understand. You're in the front line, and a doctor can only follow up. But I still say that your first action should always be to administer ergotine. You can give him the mixture to drink or, in the case of a bad haemorrhage, dissolve a grain of the ergotine in water and inject two minims hypodermically. The drug makes the blood vessels contract and should usually stop the bleeding.'

'Perhaps the bleeding would stop anyway,' replied Fanny, 'and ergotine injections sometimes give Louis abscesses. Anyway, it certainly helps me to do something other than just stand there and watch him. Louis is so brave. Do you know, when he was choking with blood one night last year, he wrote out a message for me: 'Don't be frightened; if this is death, it is an easy one.' Easy for Louis, perhaps, but terrifying for me.'

All this time I was aware of Lloyd standing in the background, leaning languidly on the mantelpiece next to an engraving of Turner's 'Bell Rock Lighthouse'. For a youth, he was unusually self-confident. He was smiling to himself, in a manner suggesting that his intellect was functioning at a higher level. The impression of arrogance was exaggerated by his tallness and by the absence of spectacles needed to correct his obvious short-sightedness. Perhaps his appearance was misleading. Certainly his academic ability was questionable: he had recently abandoned Edinburgh and the study of engineering in favour of a proposed holiday in the West Indies. I could not understand him for the simple reason that I had not known him before he reached that difficult age, the age of 17, the age that surrounds itself with a fog of uncertainty and mystery. How different it is with our own children, observed from the first day, long before any defences are put up, so that we can see into their souls, as though looking through glass, with an intimacy that no other relationship (least of all marriage) could survive.

Lloyd spoke. 'The other thing is that Louis doesn't accept he's got consumption: he talks about his ailment as if it were an enigma.'

Of course, I was aware that Louis didn't regard himself as consumptive. I knew that the diagnosis was a matter of debate, and I also knew that Fanny didn't wish to debate it.

I fiddled with the lock on my medical bag, which was still resting awkwardly on my knees. 'There's no need for us to dwell on the diagnosis. Treatment is more important.'

Fanny responded immediately with a question. 'As far as treatment is concerned, have you read the July 18th copy of *The Lancet*?'

I hesitated, trying to recall if I had read anything that might be relevant to Louis's case. I knew that Fanny had subscribed to *The Lancet* for at least a couple of years. She had the habit of picking out articles from the journal and 'fitting' the details around her husband's symptoms in a way which could be alarming as well as misleading. I believe that intelligent patients should be given enough technical information for them to understand the rationale of treatment, but the fact is that I had only recently started reading the journal myself, in an attempt to keep one move ahead of Fanny. To be honest, I still find many of *The Lancet* articles difficult to understand, and often irrelevant to General Practice.

'I mean the leading article on the use of cocaine in hay fever,' added Fanny excitedly. 'According to *The Lancet*, the value of this wonderful remedy is only just beginning to be appreciated. Apparently, a cocaine tablet in each nostril will relieve nasal congestion and breathlessness immediately and completely. Louis's symptoms always begin with nasal congestion and catarrh. Do you think that we should use cocaine?'

'Perhaps we should consider it,' I replied, making a mental note to read the relevant copy of *The Lancet* as soon as possible. 'I'm always willing to try out new treatments, but I don't like to be too experimental. For the time being, I suggest sticking with morphine for his cough. He likes the camphorated opium tincture.'

'Okay. The other thing is that colds always set off his catarrh and fever. I have a theory that colds are contagious, and I intend to keep anyone who has a cold well away from Louis. Of course this will annoy some of his literary friends but that can't be helped. In any case, I've decided to limit all visits to quarter of an hour at present. Louis gets so tired and, if you give him a chance, he'll talk too much for his own good.'

I knew all about Fanny's habit of standing with a watch outside Louis's bedroom door when he had a visitor, ready to let them know when their time was up. After all, this was done in my name, on 'doctor's orders'. And why should I object to that? Fanny was prepared, perhaps eager, to make herself unpopular with some of Louis's friends because she wanted to protect him from himself, from his love of conversation and disputation. It was my job to encourage her.

'I doubt that your theories of contagion have any medical or scientific basis, Mrs. Stevenson. However, you can rely on me to support your decisions at all times, because what you're doing is in the best interests of his health, and that's what concerns me. Certainly, if he has any blood spitting he must rest and speak only in a whisper, if at all; put his right arm in a sling to keep that lung as still as possible, and keep all visitors away.'

'I'm so relieved to hear you say that. After all, it was when Louis's friends Henley and Baxter visited us in the south of

France that things got really bad. They insisted on taking him on their 'Riviera run' to Monaco and Nice, not realising, or not caring to realise, that whenever he gets a slight cold he can become gravely ill in a matter of days. All they wanted was the pleasure of Louis's company without taking any responsibility for his health. I made up my mind there and then to protect Louis from his friends, however much they might resent my actions.'

I knew that Fanny had achieved unpopularity with many of Louis's friends. She radiated a determined possessiveness that seemed to grow stronger by the day. And she was becoming more domesticated, taking a pride in her house and garden, the pride of ownership which her husband claimed to despise but on which he depended. Sitting there in her dining room, her 'Blue Room', with her china on display, with her new furniture in place, and with a fire blazing in the grate, she was at home. The son standing next to her, blinking myopically, simply emphasised the force of her personality. I was happy to be an ally of Mrs. R.L. Stevenson.

Chapter Twelve

LOUIS WAS IN BED half propped up on a pile of pillows, his papers in front of him, books strewn over the bedclothes and floor. His long hair straggled over the top of the red poncho, which gave a mysterious quality to the shape of his body. His face was thin, his light brown moustache untrimmed and his complexion paler than usual, but his eyes were alight with welcome.

'My dear Scott, you see that I am obeying your instructions to stay in bed until Bluidy Jack has been well and truly vanquished.'

Louis habitually referred to blood spitting as 'Bluidy Jack', both in speech and in writing, perhaps because he wanted to invest his enemy with the character of a pirate, or perhaps because he couldn't spell 'haemorrhage'. I knew that 'Bluidy Jack' was not likely to be vanquished, but perhaps he might be contained by our old friends, time and rest.

'Exactly right, Stevenson, exactly right. Let's treat our foes with respect.'

Louis smiled, glancing sideways at me in mock dismissiveness, and then quietly extinguishing a cigarette between his thumb and forefinger. He had developed the ability of rolling the thinnest of thin cigarettes, always using Papier Persan from Paris, but he couldn't disguise the fact that they contained tobacco.

'You're right, of course, Scott. I should give up this delicious habit for good and all. There's little point in repeatedly stopping smoking, as I do, when one's true motive in prolonging the period of abstinence is merely to intensify the joy of starting again.'

'I can't say that there's any medical reason to advise against smoking tobacco,' I replied. 'I only say that moderation of the habit is difficult to achieve. That's what imprisons a man. And abstinence has its own rewards.'

'If you say so, then I'm sure that you believe it. But look at it from my point of view. Anything that helps mental concentration must be good for my work. I need to earn money, Scott, to keep the bailiffs from the door. For a man of nearly 35 to be financially dependent on his father is humiliating: doubly humiliating when only his wife is entrusted with the money. I've ground away at literature for so many years now, and what do I have to show for it? Just a few hundred pounds.'

'What about *Treasure Island*? Your name is known for that.'

'Not well known, really. The story was serialised under a pseudonym, and when it eventually came out in book form a couple of years ago I had to be satisfied with a hundred pounds. I was delighted – ecstatic – when the money arrived, but since then I've discovered that a hundred pounds doesn't take a married man with a stepson very far. And the book hasn't sold that well, you know: only five thousand copies in the first year. It's just a story for boys and will probably sink without trace.'

I knew well enough that Louis had financial problems. I had an outstanding bill dating back several months with the Stevensons. Most likely this would be paid in due course; if it wasn't, then I would not press for payment, would not even send a reminder. The same age as Louis, I looked upon him as my friend more than as a patient. I would happily have continued visiting him without charging any fees, if only for the pleasure of the delightful conversation that emerged between periods of what he called 'dry rot'. At that time, however, 'dry rot' prevailed.

'When you talk about imprisonment, my dear Scott, think of me here in 'Skerryvore'. A pleasant place, perhaps, but a prison none the less. And when the prisoner attempted to escape, he got no further than Exeter before reaching death's door. I was turned back at that door. My reprieve, however, was conditional: I must return to captivity. Is there any purpose in this?'

'Creativity is your purpose and your destiny.' As I write down this phrase, it appears trite, but it was spoken with an irresistible sense of compassion.

'Noble and flattering words indeed, but it's a struggle to produce anything worthwhile, despite hours of work each day.' Louis explained that he was writing a book called *Kidnapped*, a tale based on the murder of Colin Campbell, just after the Jacobite rebellion of 1745. It was an adventure story that he hoped would please his father more than anyone else. He'd started writing it at the beginning of the year, but ground to a halt by springtime, despite the fact that he'd been offered 15 shillings a column for its serialisation in *Young Folks*. 'I haven't yet had the courage to return to the story, simply because I know it will take another four or five months of hard labour to complete it. You see how feeble your patient has become.'

'Now, Stevenson, I know that you've produced other books this year.'

'Well, it's true that my *Child's Garden of Verses* has at last been published, but of course I've been working on that for years, and in any case it will appeal only to my family and friends. And *The Dynamiter* tales were written with Fanny's help, much of it in Hyères. The fact is that illness has dragged me down. In terms of simple arithmetic, I'm not producing enough work to pay the bills, including yours, my dear Scott.'

'Don't worry about my bills. I'm happy to give you what help I can, on the basis of friendship. Let's improve your health and put you on your feet again: then you really will start producing more stories. Perhaps we should get another specialist opinion?'

'No, no, please, no. I shall get damnably confused if we do that. Lauder Brunton in London told me that my lungs were seriously affected and that I should return to Davos. Dobell here in Bournemouth told me that Davos was the last place on earth that I should go to, whatever he meant by that. I'll be guided by you, Scott, and not – begging your pardon – by experts. What advice must I follow to regain good health?'

I pursed my lips, unable to disguise a feeling of irritation at the pronouncements of my distinguished colleagues. Dobell had known about the consultation with Lauder Brunton, and yet he had produced a diametrically opposite opinion, almost it seemed as a matter of principle. There are times when the practice of medicine appears to be nothing more than a gigantic bluff, with the greatest success going to the greatest bluffer. As a General Practitioner, I would prefer my specialist colleagues to show more consistency and less bravado.

'Stevenson, let me say frankly that I don't know the answer to that. Lauder Brunton is a highly respected London physician with a reputation second to none, save perhaps that of Sir Andrew Clark himself. Dobell is now a Bournemouth man, but for a long time he was physician to the Royal Hospital for Diseases of the Chest in London; he moved here two or three years ago because of a domestic tragedy, and I must say that he has energetically built up a large private practice, with many devoted patients. He has strong views: perhaps no bad thing for a physician.'

'Perhaps it is no bad thing,' replied Louis, 'provided that the strong views are correct. I have to say, though, that he does appear to be a man of some wisdom. I certainly appreciate his advice not to return to Davos, and I'm grateful to him for that. I also owe him a debt of gratitude for sending me a complimentary copy of his book *On Loss of Weight, Blood Spitting and Lung Disease*. A stomach-churning and bloodthirsty tale to rival *Treasure Island*, you might say, but I must have a word with him sometime about his literary style.'

I laughed out loud, having only recently waded through Dobell's high-flown account of his 'many definite opinions on these subjects of such stirring interest and vast practical importance'.

'I think I know what you mean. Anyway, I'm glad to hear that you've ruled out a return to Davos.'

Dobell still believes that the invigorating effect of high altitude amounts to nothing more than 'deeply ingrained and popular twaddle', to quote his words. He maintains that you only have to look at the number of cases of consumption in Greenland to realise that a cold climate cannot be beneficial. On the other hand, the Bournemouth air has all the aseptic properties of the Alpine atmosphere without the drawbacks of excessive cold and low oxygen content.

'Bournemouth may be the best prison for a man with your condition, Stevenson.'

'Condition? Do I have consumption or not?' asked Louis quietly.

'My dear fellow,' I replied, 'I'm only a simple General Practitioner.'

'General Practitioner you may be, but simple you are not. Anyway, regardless of your true opinion, you'd better not cross swords with 'Doctor' Fanny Stevenson. She believes that genius, or so-called genius, feeds off consumption, and that is that; I must write under the influence of the white plague, as if my name was Keats or Brontë. It seems to me a strange idea that shining eyes are thought to be a sign of the disease, but I don't care to dwell on the matter. Speaking personally, the only enemy that I fear is the ordinary cold, with its fiendish allies catarrh, bronchitis and blood spitting. Dr. Clark understood that and he found no signs of consumption. Why can't I see him again?'

'Sir Andrew is a busy man, Stevenson: a baronet's time is not necessarily his own. I believe that he's been away for a few weeks, accompanying Mr. Gladstone on a Norwegian cruise. Some patients are more important than others. You shouldn't complain: it's well known that Gladstone has read *Treasure Island* over and over again. Perhaps it was Clark who introduced him to your work.'

Louis snorted. 'Perhaps so, and perhaps if Gladstone had spent more time on affairs of state instead of reading boys' stories then he might still be Prime Minister. A man in his position who felt no sense of shame at the death of General Gordon is not a man that I want amongst my readership.'

I remained silent, startled by the anger of this reaction. Louis's inherited hatred of Liberalism was not an emotion that engaged my sympathy.

After a brief pause, Louis, again calm and smiling, enquired: 'Shall I bring you up to date on my shilling shocker?'

Sitting in the wicker chair at Louis's bedside, I leaned forwards towards him, listening attentively. Involuntarily, slowly, my right hand rose to cover my mouth. Less than a couple of weeks earlier, I had called early one morning to find the author in bed, writing furiously. 'I've got my shilling shocker', Louis had said, referring to the urgent financial necessity of producing the shocker that his publishers had demanded for the Christmas trade. Within three days he had written, at phenomenal speed, something he called *Strange Case of Dr. Jekyll and Mr. Hyde*, and had then destroyed the thirty thousand word manuscript, only to rewrite it within another three days. During that time, interruptions by his physician, and even by his wife, were not encouraged. I knew that Louis had dreamt the key scenes of the story, and that he had started writing at daybreak, a 'fine bogey tale' as he had described it, a tale of physical transformation between good and evil. It was the extraordinary speed and intensity of writing that had staggered me. Ten thousand words a day for three days, and then for another three days, from a writer who could sometimes spend hours agonising over a single sentence.

'It was my Brownies that got me going.' Louis was referring to the creatures that had inhabited his dreams since childhood, working away in his mind whilst he slept. 'I dreamt three scenes of the tale as clear as anything, and would have dreamt more if Fanny hadn't woken me. She should have let me scream on, as anyone who witnessed the transformation scene would and should have screamed. I dreamt of the powder, mixed and effervescing in the graduated glass with a few minims of the red tincture, which the evil Hyde took to transform himself, by a process hideous to watch, into Dr. Jekyll.'

Louis, agitated and speaking rapidly, reached for his cigarette papers and tobacco. Rolling a thin, untidy cigarette and lighting it as he talked, he turned and looked directly at me.

'It was the worst of nightmares, but as soon as I was awake I knew that I had to write it out of myself. That's why I scribbled so furiously for three days, and that's why I couldn't give you more than a few minutes of my time: I was too busy to be ill.' Held between his right forefinger and middle finger, the cigarette burned slowly, its plume of smoke revealing a fine tremor of the hand. Such delicate hands, such unusually long, thin fingers, without any suggestion of that club-like appearance which is sometimes associated with lung disease.

'What about your act of destruction, Stevenson? Why did you burn the manuscript and then immediately rewrite the story?'

'After I'd finished the first draft, I was both exhilarated and exhausted. You can imagine my disappointment when I saw Fanny's face register disapproval as I was reading it to her. I was upset by her criticism, more upset than I would have been by the strictures of a literary critic. In fact, I was not merely upset, I was in a rage. Poor Lloyd, who'd been listening to the story as well – and listening with a splendid, wide-eyed, horrified attentiveness – had to leave the room, unable to bear the pain of witnessing a first rate, blazing row between his mother and myself. That is what led me to burn the manuscript. I probably shocked Fanny but I rewrote it in another three days, producing I think a better version; as usual, the judgement of the Wild Woman of the West was correct.'

'And the red mixture in the minim glass. Not ergotine I hope?'

'No, no,' replied Louis, laughing. 'Ergotine can make me sick, it can make me thirsty, it can make me dizzy, it can make my hands and feet tingle, but it can't transform me into Dr.

Jekyll, nor into Mr. Hyde for that matter. I can assure you, Scott, that your medicines are not Jekyll's medicines. These days, even morphine does no more than dull me.'

'The laudanum that I prescribe for your cough only contains a small percentage of morphine, you know. You're not likely to become a De Quincey on the amount that we allow you.'

'I prefer the evil of the tobacco weed to that of the poppy,' replied Louis. 'Nightmares have been my companions since childhood. I don't need any artificial dreams.'

'And Dr. Jekyll, Stevenson. Not myself, I hope?' I shifted uncomfortably on the creaking wicker seat of the chair as I hesitantly asked him this question. Needless to say, nothing would have delighted me more than to feature as one of the characters in a Stevenson tale.

'Certainly not,' replied Louis. 'Jekyll is nobody, and he is everybody. Don't expect to identify him, but you may be interested in the personality of Dr. Lanyon, Jekyll's more distinguished colleague. All will be revealed soon. I just need a couple more weeks to polish the narrative, and then the book should be on sale by Christmas. With bankruptcy at my heels, I can run like a hare!'

Bankruptcy, for Louis, was not a real risk: he was shielded by his father's wealth. And yet I could but admire his desperate desire for financial independence. I marvelled that he had somehow found the inner strength to write at such a pace, after so many months of stagnation. What sort of illness was it that allowed him to do this? Was this the feverish creative urge that we sometimes see in consumption? If so, why had he produced so little during the previous few months of illness? Or was he a man who, regardless of illness or health, carried beneath his flippant exterior an iron determination to succeed at his chosen trade, to prove to his father that at last he was his own man? Whatever the explanation might be, the intense emotional energy that Louis had injected into his 'shilling shocker' would surely produce a book of rare insight, good enough to earn him public recognition and to make his father proud of him. I was more than confident that, for myself and for many others, this would be a shilling well spent.

Chapter Thirteen

IT WAS TOWARDS THE end of 1886 that I got to know Thomas Stevenson, or at least the fading shadow of the man. At that time, Thomas and Maggie were living in a rented house in Bournemouth, and so it was to be expected that they would spend many hours at 'Skerryvore', sometimes sitting with Louis, sometimes waiting patiently for him to appear.

Of course, I had not known Thomas in the prime of his life, but it was easy enough to imagine what a formidable force he must have been. In repose, his facial features suggested granite-like strength, his steady gaze incorruptible honesty. When he began to speak, however, it was the speech of a man unsure of himself: hesitant, mumbling, sometimes trailing off into nothingness. Unable to find the word that he wanted, he would pick an inappropriate alternative, and then another and another, until frustration gave way to anger; sometimes he would even curse, using words which Maggie had never before heard him utter. At the age of 68, he appeared to be degenerating into senility, struggling in vain against the softening of his brain. It was a scenario all too familiar to me in my professional life as a Bournemouth doctor, but not one to which I could relate in a personal way. My own father, a doctor, died at the age of 46, leaving a widow with 14 children to support and much more to worry about than the vagaries of old age.

I never saw Thomas alone, even for a professional consultation. Maggie was her husband's constant companion, seeming to need him as much as he needed her. There were times when she could be too helpful, finding words for him before he had lost them, but in general she was a superb judge of his needs, weaknesses and strengths. She had the advantage of being ten years younger than her husband, in a curious mirror image of Fanny's ten year seniority over Louis.

In contrast to Thomas's increasing slowness of speech and movement, Maggie was alert, attentive and sharp. Briskly cheerful, especially when her husband's mood was low, she gave the impression of being able to cope with any setback. Unlike Thomas, she had never shown any tendency to gain weight; coming up to her 58th birthday, she still retained the neat, slim figure of her youth.

I found Thomas and Maggie in the drawing room of 'Skerryvore'. It was the room that Louis used most often for writing, and there were books and papers piled, seemingly at random, on the table. Although the writer himself was not there, his familiar image was on the wall: a portrait painted at 'Skerryvore' by John Singer Sargent, showing Louis as an emaciated, long-fingered, long-legged, pacing figure, a restless spirit with a brilliant intensity of gaze. To my mind, that portrait fails to show the gentle side of Louis, but judges more expert than myself have decreed that his true personality is there, on the canvas, for all to see.

Maggie bustled across the room and gripped me by the elbow: a friendly, conspiratorial grip. 'Louis isn't up yet, Dr. Scott, but I'm sure that he'd be glad to see you.'

'It's only a social call, really, Mrs. Stevenson, and I should have sent a message that I was coming to see him. I quite understand his dislike of unexpected calls, even from his doctor.'

'Well, you're as much a friend to him as a doctor. Now please tell me, do you think that he's getting any better?'

I knew that optimism would be misleading. In May, after Louis had finished writing *Kidnapped*, Dobell had diagnosed 'brain exhaustion', and advised a change of scene. Spitting blood in June, Louis had delayed a journey to London and Paris until August. Buoyed up by the success of this trip, he had then returned to London in October, only to be laid low by a cold and more blood spitting. Summoned from Bournemouth, I had been more than pleased to help him, and flattered to be consulted in preference to London doctors. All in all, however, Dobell's recommended 'change of scene' had not been spectacularly successful.

'He's better than he was in October,' I replied, 'and his fighting spirit in the face of adversity is a lesson to all of us.'

As soon as I had spoken these words, I regretted that I had even opened my mouth. Thomas appeared to descend deeper into his personal despair. He remained silent.

'Mr. Stevenson, sir, how do you find Louis?' I could not prevent myself from adopting a loud, jolly tone.

'Frail, frail. As are we all.'

Maggie interrupted before he could take this gloomy theme any further. 'Believe me, it's wonderful for us to be able to see Louis so often. I hope we're not interrupting his work, but he does want to do everything he can to help his father. Of course you'll know that they went together to Matlock in April: a twosome just as in the days of Louis's childhood! I was so pleased for both of them.'

I knew from Louis's own account that the trip to Smedley's Hydropathic at Matlock Bridge had been something less than a success. Thomas had acquiesced in the curious regime of lukewarm vinegar sponging, hot mustard baths and so on, but he had been garrulous and argumentative, forever picking on some trivial matter and refusing to let it go. Perhaps Maggie had forgotten that she had been summoned to join her husband and son, to calm the atmosphere.

'The only problem in Matlock,' she went on, 'was the news of Bogue's death. I think it reminded Louis how sad he'd been at the loss of Coolin, the Skye terrier of his childhood.'

Perhaps so, although I cannot say that Bogue was a friend of mine, nor of any visitor to 'Skerryvore'. To my mind, his death in a dogfight was a fitting end for a warrior.

'We all miss Bogue,' I replied. A true statement but at the same time dishonest.

Thomas pulled at his watch chain, and then pulled and pulled again. This distinguished civil engineer, this builder of famous lighthouses, was unable to complete the task of extracting the watch from the pocket of his waistcoat; Maggie did it for him, and simultaneously, deftly, brushed a few crumbs off his jacket with her other hand. Thomas studied the face of the elegant gold timepiece as if it were the page of a book. I didn't know whether this signified impatience – with Louis, or myself – or whether his mind was elsewhere, or nowhere.

'How does it feel to be the father of a celebrated author?' I asked him gaily, anxious to retain his attention but uncertain how he would react to any question, however innocuous. '*Jekyll and Hyde* seems to be going from success to success.'

This was an understatement. The publication of *Jekyll and Hyde* in January had been followed closely by an excellent review in *The Times*. The book had then become the subject of a sermon by a canon at St. Paul's Cathedral, and subsequently the subject of many sermons throughout the land. I was one of the first in Bournemouth to buy a copy of the 'shilling shocker' which, with the 25 per cent discount that the retailer allowed, actually cost me only ninepence, a modest enough price for a book of 149 pages, nicely bound in light brown paper covers with brightly coloured titling.

I was not the only one to hand over my ninepence or a shilling. Within six months of publication, the book sold forty thousand copies in Great Britain, and many more in the USA. It was in this way that Louis became an author with a celebrated name and, earning twopence on every copy sold, an author with money to pay into the bank.

It was indeed a shocker of a tale, the evil at its core strangely disconcerting to one such as myself. As Louis had promised, the characters of Jekyll and Hyde appeared to be entirely imaginary. There was, however, no difficulty in identifying the origin of Jekyll's friend and colleague, Dr. Lanyon.

> With that he blew out his candle, put on a great coat, and set forth in the direction of Cavendish Square, that citadel of medicine, where his friend, the great Dr. Lanyon, had his house and received his crowding patients... The geniality, as was the way of the man, was somewhat theatrical to the eye; but it reposed on genuine feeling.

How would Sir Andrew Clark react to this thinly disguised portrayal of himself? I could only hope that his excellent health would not be disturbed by the merciless description of Dr. Lanyon's demise later in the story:

> He had his death-warrant written legibly upon his face. The rosy man had grown pale; his flesh had fallen away;

he was visibly balder and older... A week afterwards Dr. Lanyon took to his bed, and in something less than a fortnight he was dead.

Thomas mournfully gave his verdict on the book: 'Yes, it's a success.'

'And it's producing a good income for Louis,' added Maggie. 'Of course, you'll know that Tom has always done everything possible to support Louis financially, without ever expecting any thanks. Louis is hopeless with money. He ran out of funds in Paris earlier this year simply because he'd forgotten about a cheque for a hundred pounds that Tom had given him. A hundred pounds! Louis had assumed that he'd already spent the money; it was Tom who noticed that the amount hadn't been debited from the bank account. Hopeless!' Maggie smiled with affection at the thought of her son's delightful ignorance of money matters.

'It's not everyone that can afford to be hopeless. If only I...I...' Thomas's voice tailed off with a grunt of frustration.

'Yes Tom?' asked Maggie, leaning forwards in her chair and holding her husband's hand. There was no reply.

'Tom has written books himself, Dr. Scott. His *Design and Construction of Harbours* was reprinted earlier this year, and his book on lighthouse illumination is still in demand. My husband is a brilliant man with an original mind. Did you know that it was Tom who invented the louvre-boarded screens used for protection of meteorological instruments?'

'No, indeed,' I replied, surprised and impressed. Thomas himself sat still, staring blankly ahead, his mouth half open, saliva coursing its way gently down his chin from the corner of his mouth.

'And *Kidnapped*, Mr. Stevenson,' I added, trying to attract Thomas's attention. '*Kidnapped* is proving to be a popular book, I understand.'

Kidnapped had been serialised in *Young Folks* from May to July, and then published in book form. In a sense, I was a participant in the creation of this famous story, for I was Louis's loyal attendant throughout much of the long drawn out effort needed to complete it. The final stages, when he seemed to lose interest in the tale, were particularly difficult, not least because of the untimely diversion provided by the Matlock trip. It's no secret that Louis brought the story to a premature close, promising to complete it with a sequel in due course. Despite all this, it was soon evident that David Balfour's adventures in the Highlands of Scotland would provide Louis with another literary and commercial success. He could no longer be described as a struggling author.

'*Kidnapped*.' Thomas, suddenly alert, regained interest in the conversation. 'Excellent book. Wonderful. He asked for my guidance on the...er...er...'

Maggie came to the rescue. 'The Earraid chapter? You see, Dr. Scott, all the details of David Balfour's four days of wandering on Earraid – that's the tidal islet off the Isle of Mull – were derived from knowledge that Louis gained from his trip there back in 1870. And that trip was for Thomas's firm: Earraid was used as a base when they were constructing the Dhu Heartach lighthouse. In fact Tom and I joined Louis on Earraid at the end of his trip. It was a wonderful time, a time when Tom still thought that Louis would become an engineer and join the family firm. In a way, *Kidnapped* has brought Louis back to his father again.'

'And Hen...Hen...' Maggie was about to intervene, but this time Thomas managed to spit out the words: 'Henderland was my idea.' In fact I already knew that Louis had introduced a religious chapter to please his father. The character of Henderland, the solemn catechist sent out from Edinburgh to evangelize the savage Highlands, was not exactly a sympathetic portrait. Certainly, Henderland's habit of desperately ladling snuff into his nose suggested a lack of self-control that, in the context, was almost comical.

As a liberal churchman, I was anxious to avoid any religious debate with such a stern Calvinist as Thomas Stevenson. I changed the subject. 'Rumour has it that Mr. Gladstone, after resigning as Prime Minister, turned to *Kidnapped* and read it in a single day.' I spoke brightly enough, but said no more than that, remembering too late the Stevenson antipathy to the Grand Old Man.

Thomas's expression darkened. There was no hesitation. 'Gladstone's third and last term, I hope. It is enough.'

It was fortunate that Louis chose this moment to join us. Bounding into the room, the lean figure appeared as cheerful as I had ever seen him, the outward signs of illness supplanted, or at least disguised, by an air of buoyant self-confidence.

I smiled with pleasure at the sight of my friend, but it was Thomas who moved first, and surprisingly quickly, to embrace Louis. 'Now come along, dearie. Come and sit with us. Did you sleep well? How are you feeling?'

Gazing fondly at his son's face, and with an arm round his shoulder, he might have been talking to a little boy. But, sadly, the tower of strength was crumbling, and it was the little boy who was beginning to look like the man of the family.

Chapter Fourteen

BEYOND SKERRYVORE'S LAWN and kitchen garden, the narrow winding path tracked down the side of the chine to a small clearing, where there was enough space for two or three seats. Here, where the sunlight was filtered by the branches and the needles of pine trees, was an area of delicious freshness, a refuge from the heat of the afternoon on that warmest of June days in 1887. I was seated between Louis and Fanny, the three of us looking lazily down and about the chine as conversation ebbed and flowed. The thickness of my jacket and waistcoat was just about tolerable, but still my body was damp with perspiration; I envied Louis his freedom to wear loose, comfortable, untidy clothing. Even so, recovering as he was from a touch of pleurisy, he shouldn't have been out of doors. Rolling a cigarette, striking a match, lighting the cigarette, passing it to Fanny, rolling and lighting another cigarette, he took a minute or two to say a few words.

'I don't think that Father would have wanted us to stay at 'Skerryvore' indefinitely, even though he bought the house for us. We have to consider the future.'

Fanny, puffing expertly on her cigarette, looked away from her husband, but said nothing. She had come to love the house, the garden and the neighbourhood. Despite her history of travelling and pioneering, she had eagerly absorbed the comforts of domesticity. She took a pride in their possessions – unlike Louis, who professed to abhor the burdens of ownership – and she had an ambition to become an important local hostess. Why should all her work on the house be sacrificed to Louis's whims? I am not saying that she was uniformly happy at 'Skerryvore'; on a number of occasions she left Bournemouth to spend a few days or weeks away from Louis. For example, during the summer of 1886 she went to London for medical treatment, returning with a long letter for me from a doctor who advised that she needed, not drugs, but a holiday at Aix-les-Bains; fortunately, for Louis's sake, I was able to put a spoke in that particular wheel. Looking back on all this, however, I feel that my concern for Louis's welfare may have overshadowed my duty to his good wife, whose tendency to develop symptoms during times when Louis was relatively well simply indicated that she needed a period of escape.

I asked Louis a direct question. 'Did your father actually say that he didn't expect you to continue living in Bournemouth?'

'Not in so many words. By the time that he left here for Edinburgh in April, he was too ill to talk about such matters. The jaundice seemed to make him even more depressed than usual.'

'That's hardly surprising,' I replied. Thomas Stevenson's last few weeks in Bournemouth were dominated by jaundice: relentlessly deepening yellowness, accompanied by constant, irritating itching, likened by Thomas to the results of an attack by West Highland midges at dusk in summertime. Cancer of the pancreas, no doubt, but of course I didn't upset the family with any overt reference to malignancy; it was enough of a burden for them to know that his death was imminent.

Fanny extinguished the stub of her cigarette between thumb and forefinger, in the style of her husband (or perhaps he had learnt it from her). 'Louis's father knew that he was dying.

That's why he went back to Edinburgh with Mrs. Stevenson. A fortnight later he was dead. At the end, he passed away in his sleep, but only a couple of days earlier he'd been up and about.'

'He always said that he wanted to smoke a pipe on his last day,' added Louis, 'and that was so nearly accomplished. The really sad thing was that, after my mother had telegraphed for me to come home, he didn't recognise me when I got there. It was pitiful to watch him, fighting to stay on his feet, as if going to bed at that stage would be an act of laziness or a sign of defeat.'

'It was all terribly difficult for Louis, Dr. Scott. He caught a cold on the way up to Edinburgh. Dr. Balfour, his uncle, told him straight out that he was too ill to go to the funeral; poor Louis had to stay at home and watch the procession leave from Heriot Row. And it was one of the largest funerals seen in Edinburgh for years, with over a hundred invited guests. It was a great tribute to the old man.'

Louis winced. 'Quite so, Fanny, quite so.'

I looked at my friend with sympathy, but not complete understanding. Had he really been too ill to go to his father's funeral? Many are the times that I have prohibited poorly patients from attending the funerals of their loved ones, but such edicts have usually been ignored; there are some occasions that transcend the pursuit of health. I feared that Louis's absence from the final tribute to his father would, inevitably and in due course, weigh heavily on his conscience.

Louis seemed to be aware of the discomfort in my mind. 'I believe that my love for Father will show through in my writing. I've already prepared an article about him, to appear in this month's *Contemporary Review*. I think it would have satisfied him: it's factual rather than sentimental. I've said that his lights are in every part of the world, guiding the mariner.'

We sat without speaking for a while, the silence broken only by the wood pigeons, 'coo-coo-cooo-c-cooo, cuk' repeatedly and gently penetrating the heat of the afternoon.

Then Fanny spoke. 'We stayed on in Edinburgh for nearly a month. There was so much to do, helping Mrs. Stevenson, and trying to sort out the estate. For weeks, Louis was ill, but Dr. Balfour looked after him really well and got him better again. And during all this time, there was no haemorrhage! It was like a small miracle.'

'Some miracle. I am in the blackest of black depression, inherited directly from my father, no doubt.'

Fanny threw her cigarette to the ground and stamped on it. Ignoring my presence, she stood up and shouted at her husband. 'Now look here, Louis, what you've inherited is financial security. Three thousand pounds for our immediate use, and capital of twenty thousand pounds due on your mother's death. Is that a cause for depression?'

'Who knows?' replied Louis. 'The tragedy is that it's come to me at the very time that I've begun to achieve financial independence as a result of my own efforts. If only Father could have lived long enough to see and to understand that! How I would have loved to pay something back to him.'

Fanny sat down again, her temper calmed as quickly as it had flared up. 'Don't blame yourself, Louis. The old man loved his work. He looked on you as a boy and was content to support you. You rewarded him with *Treasure Island* and *Kidnapped*.'

'Perhaps so. In any case, now we must look to the future.

Uncle George says that my lungs are in need of repair. He has issued a decree that we must go to the mountains of Colorado for the winter. Bluidy Jack won't necessarily leave me, but in the New World my health can and will improve.'

'And so I must wrench myself away from our Bournemouth nest,' added Fanny.

'Tell me, my dear Scott,' asked Louis, 'what is your opinion?

My opinion was that Dr. George Balfour had stepped well outside the bounds of acceptable professional etiquette in casting doubt on colleagues' advice, and adopting a dictatorial attitude. It was as if the Edinburgh physician had said: 'You can now forget everything you've been told about your medical condition, and I'll put you right.' And yet this didn't involve any day-to-day or long term commitment from Dr. Balfour himself; his advice, put simply, was that Louis should go to another continent.

Of course, I did not give my true opinion: that would have been hurtful to Louis. 'The mountain air again? Would it work this time? I don't think that Dobell would approve. And would it suit Fanny's health? I'm not sure...'

Fortunately, Fanny interrupted me as I floundered. 'Don't worry about me. I can cope with it, as long as it's good for Louis's health. He's desperate to go, to get away. He can afford to travel in more comfort now, and he no longer needs to stay within reach of his father. As for his mother, well, he wants her to come with us. It's as good as arranged.'

I was beginning to suspect that my friend had cajoled his uncle into giving the advice that he wanted to hear. Perhaps I had misjudged Dr. Balfour.

'Well, if that's what you want, Stevenson, then of course you have my support and good wishes. Who am I to speak against travel for the sake of health? My own trip to Tasmania as a young man was a life saver.'

Louis flashed a smile at me. 'It's settled then. We need to go in August, to get the best weather for the Atlantic crossing. Lloyd will come with us, of course – I couldn't manage without his company now – and perhaps our maid Valentine as well.'

'What about your butler?' I asked him, teasingly. Since the Stevensons had returned from Edinburgh, they had employed a new member of staff: a butler, who appeared to be more decorative than useful. I doubted that a butler would be willing to stay for long in that chaotic household, whatever the family plans might be.

Louis blushed gracefully. 'I think not,' he replied.

With such talk of buttling, Fanny decided that it was time for her to organise some tea for us. Left alone with Louis, silence for a few moments was comfortable; I felt completely at ease in his company.

When at last he chose to speak, it was in a low, trembling voice. 'I can't see that I'll recover from my father's decline and death, unless I go abroad.'

'I understand, my friend,' I replied.

'Do you? I doubt it. You think too well of me. You don't see that I am more Hyde than Jekyll.'

'Don't be ridiculous, Stevenson. You're experiencing a perfectly natural sense of grief and depression.'

Louis smiled, not in a pleasant way.

'You know about the dream that led to the story of Jekyll and Hyde, but I've never told you about an even more powerful nightmare of my earlier life. Let me tell you about it now.'

He stood and looked away from me, down the chine, as he spoke.

'I dreamt that I'd lived abroad for many years, to escape my father. When at last I returned home, I found that he'd married again and was treating his young wife cruelly. I refused to visit him, but we agreed to meet on a remote sandy shore; there we quarrelled, and I killed him. My crime was undetected, and so I inherited his fortune and moved into the family house, to live with his widow. I was attracted to her, but somehow I knew that she suspected my guilt. One day she travelled to the sandy shore. I followed her there and watched her find a vital piece of evidence, which so shocked her that she slipped and was in peril of her life, forcing me to reveal myself, to save her. She kept the evidence, but wouldn't denounce me. Day by day, the burden of suspense grew more unbearable, so that I began to waste away like a man with a disease. Eventually, in a torment of guilt, I ransacked her room, found the evidence and demanded to know why she tortured me, why she wouldn't denounce me. Then she fell to her knees with arms outstretched: 'Do you not understand?' she cried, 'I love you.' That, Scott, was the point at which I awoke. And now tell me, what does it mean?'

'I haven't the foggiest idea,' I replied. 'Perhaps it means that your imagination works overtime. Clearly, the father in your dreams was not your father. In real life, he loved you, and you loved him.'

'As you say, my dear Scott, as you say.'

Then it was that Fanny reappeared, walking slowly down the path. Close behind her, dressed in black and illuminated by speckled sunlight, came the butler, carrying a tray of tea and cakes.

'This is the life, Louis,' she called out.
'As you say, Fanny, as you say.'

* * * * *

In October 1887, two months after Louis had left Bournemouth, his volume of poetry, *Underwoods*, was published with a dedication to certain members of the medical profession, most notably myself. I reproduce this here below. If humility and pride can live together in one soul, then that explains my feelings whenever I read these lines.

There are men and classes of men that stand above the common herd: the soldier, the sailor and the shepherd not unfrequently; the artist rarely; rarelier still, the clergyman; the physician almost as a rule. He is the flower (such as it is) of our civilisation; and when that stage of man is done with, and only remembered to be marvelled at in history, he will be thought to have shared as little as any in the defects of the period, and most notably exhibited the virtues of the race. Generosity he has, such as is possible to those who practise an art, never to those who drive a trade; discretion, tested by a hundred secrets; tact, tried in a thousand embarrassments; and, what are more important, Heraclean cheerfulness and courage. So it is that he brings air and cheer into the sick room, and often enough, though not so often as he wishes, brings healing.

Gratitude is but a lame sentiment; thanks, when they are expressed, are often more embarrassing than welcome; and yet I must set forth mine to a few out of many doctors who have brought me comfort and help; to Dr. Willey of San Francisco, whose kindness to a stranger it must be as grateful to him, as it is touching to me, to remember; to Dr. Karl Ruedi of Davos, the good genius of the English in his frosty mountains; to Dr. Herbert of Paris, whom I knew only for a week, and to Dr. Caissot of Montpellier, whom I knew only for ten days, and who have yet written their names deeply in my memory; to Dr. Brandt of Royat; to Dr. Wakefield of Nice; to Dr. Chepmell, whose visits make it a pleasure to be ill; to Dr. Horace Dobell, so wise in counsel; to Sir Andrew Clark, so unwearied in kindness; and to that wise youth, my uncle, Dr. Balfour.

I forget as many as I remember; and I ask both to pardon me, these for silence, those for inadequate speech. But one name I have kept on purpose to the last, because it is a household word with me, and because if I had not received favours from so many hands and in so many quarters of the world, it should have stood upon this page alone: that of my friend Thomas Bodley Scott of Bournemouth. Will he accept this, although shared among so many, for a dedication to himself? And when next my ill-fortune (which has thus its pleasant side) brings him hurrying to me when he would fain sit down to meat or lie down to rest, will he care to remember that he takes this trouble for one who is not fool enough to be ungrateful?

Part Four:
Dr. E.L. Trudeau's Narrative

Chapter Fifteen

I AM AS FAMILIAR as any man can be with the rigorous climate of the Adirondack Mountains. In 1887, when Louis arrived here, I had already lived in the Saranac Lake region of New York State for 14 years, and had hunted deer, hare and fox. Even for the Adirondacks, however, December of that year was decidedly cold, with the temperature already dipping to 20 degrees below zero, and set to plunge further as the depth of the winter approached.

It was a ten minute walk from Saranac Lake village up the hill to Baker's Cottage, where the Stevensons were lodged for the winter. Trudging through the snow and weighed down by my heavy coat, I was breathing heavily as I came to the end of my short journey. There, pacing up and down the verandah at the front of the cottage, was Louis. An instantly recognisable figure, despite being bulked out by an ankle-length buffalo skin coat, and his head covered by a dark-fleeced Astrakhan cap. His every breath formed a cone of mist in the raw atmosphere.

I made a point of walking up to see Louis every few days. Not necessarily to give professional advice. My visits acknowledged the author's status as an important, valued patient, a man who could attract welcome publicity for Saranac Lake. It was fortunate that the Stevensons had decided against the long journey to Colorado and in favour of the lower altitude Adirondacks. I do not need to point out that Saranac Lake represents everything that is most up-to-date in the treatment of consumption. In those days, however, there was an urgent need to attract funds for my developing 'cottage' sanatorium. We needed to provide a healthy environment and good treatment for patients too poor to rent their own accommodation in the area. To this end, a famous patient, whose every move was reported in the New York papers, was a gift to be prized and cultivated. I make no apology for using those who are well off to help those who are disadvantaged.

'Is it cold enough for you yet, Stevenson?' was my greeting to him as I stepped up on to the verandah of the cottage. A simple wooden frame house, its dulled whiteness offset by bright green shutters and a red tiled roof.

'20 degrees below freezing point and still falling, according to *The Quarterly Reviewer*.' This was his nickname for the thermometer that hung from a nail, hammered at a jaunty angle into one of the verandah posts.

'Sorry your walks are restricted by bad weather at present. The same view day after day can be irksome.'

'Trudeau, there's really no such thing as bad weather, you know. Only different kinds of good weather. That is, according to the words of John Ruskin, spoken I suspect during a period of unusual optimism. It may be grey and freezing, but I haven't had a cold or catarrh since I arrived. That's certainly good from my point of view.'

Words of commendation for Saranac Lake! And yes, of course, the view from the house was not really the same day after day. Varieties of cloud formation, light and shade could paint a picture which danced and changed minute by minute.

Louis stood at the edge of the verandah with arms outspread.

'This could be a Scottish hillside. Pine trees dressed with snow, the river churning and racing through the valley. It's Perthshire at a lower temperature. I think that's why I spend so much time walking up and down these plain timber boards. You may not understand this, Trudeau, but in reality I'm thinking and working all the time. This is already a place of comfort and familiarity for me, a place which encourages ideas to bob up in my mind, sometimes ideas which have been dormant for many years. It was on this verandah, on a frosty night not many weeks ago, that I started writing, in my mind, a story.' Louis was referring to *The Master of Ballantrae*. 'It's a tale that began with my winter walk in Carrick and Galloway more than a decade ago, a tale half thought out on the moors between Pitlochry and Strathardle four or five years later, a tale remembered and now at last coming to fruition in this wooden cottage on a snowy hillside.' He let his arms fall and hang down loosely. 'Does any of this make sense to a scientist, Trudeau?'

'This particular scientist can't wait so many years before working on his ideas.' My reply was brisk. I was speaking to a man much touched by illness, a man only two years younger than myself, but I doubted that he was well-versed in suffering. At the time of the Stevenson walk in Carrick and Galloway, I was already settled into the Adirondacks. I chose Saranac Lake because of my love of the outdoor life, and my belief that this was a place where I could learn to acquiesce in my death. I am referring to a death of slow pace, from the consumption that struck me soon after my graduation from Medical School. Not that my illness was recognised during my year as a House Physician in New York. At that time my exhaustion was put down to the pressure of unremitting work at the Strangers'

Hospital. On my first day as a House Physician I was unceremoniously thrown in at the deep end: I was put in charge of all
the wards, without any experience whatsoever of treating serious disease. It is difficult to explain the sense of bewilderment
and inadequacy that accompanies the sudden transition from
feckless student to trusted doctor. I was ill, but the poor patients
of that hospital suffered far more than I did. And then I was on
honeymoon in Europe, still unwell, still with undiagnosed consumption. I was seen by a self-satisfied Liverpool physician who
told me that I was 'run down', that I needed more bacon for
breakfast. So much for the scientific basis of English medicine!
And then I was in medical practice on Long Island for a year,
when my fever was put down to malaria and treated with quinine. My illness was recognised as consumption only when I saw
Dr. Janeway, that brilliant New York diagnostician; he told me,
using the fewest number of words possible, that the upper two
thirds of my left lung was tuberculous. I chose to die at Saranac
Lake; during whatever time was left for me, I wanted the beauty of the forests and hills, and the simple life of the hunter.
Several years elapsed before the realisation dawned that my
health was improving, not deteriorating. In this way it emerged
that the climate of the Adirondacks might prove to be as beneficial to consumptives as that of the newly fashionable Alpine
resorts. I restarted medical practice and gradually built up the
reputation of Saranac Lake as an area ideally suited to the treatment of consumption. All my careerist energies, which had lain
dormant during the years of illness, became focused, with an
intensity unimaginable to a younger man, on the conquest of
this disease. And so you will understand that, at the age of 39,
and with this history, I could not indulge myself in the luxury of

waiting for ideas to 'bob up' before starting work at my desk or bench.

I strode ahead of Louis as we moved round the back of the house to get in through the kitchen door. I could feel, running down from my nostrils, two rivulets, slowing and freezing on my walrus moustache. Such trivial things invariably enhance my self-consciousness, which is so firmly embedded in my rather strange egg-shaped head.

'Smells like rabbit for lunch today,' remarked Louis, as we went into the kitchen, passing the large barrel of washing water, which was replenished daily by a boy carrying full pails up from the river on a neck yoke. 'A welcome change from venison and salmon trout.'

'And easier to hunt than the deer, provided that you've got a good hound,' I replied. 'Four pounds eight and a half ounces is my own best sized rabbit to date.'

'Spare me the details, Trudeau. Those of us who eat rabbit don't necessarily want to hear the executioner's tale.'

The kitchen was a scene of activity, with the cook and the maid fussing round the oven, saucepans bubbling on the stove, provisions piled untidily on the rough, homely wooden table. Louis, taking several minutes to get his hat and coat off, exchanged friendly greetings with his servants before leading me through into the sitting room.

Like almost everything else at Saranac Lake, the sitting room and its furniture, even the footstools, were made of wood. It was a room of honest, Spartan appearance, dominated by a blazing log fire in a generous sized fireplace. Louis and I joined Maggie, so that the three of us were sitting in a row directly in front of the fire, our faces glowing, our hands warm, our backs ice-cold.

Louis was apologetic. 'The kitchen's chaotic. We need Fanny back to restore an element of order. And she's a better cook than the cook.'

I hadn't seen much of Fanny before her departure for an extended trip to New York. It was said that she hated the climate of the Adirondacks, and that she had agreed to the move for one reason only: the belief that it would be good for her husband's health. And so here was Louis sitting by the fireside next to his mother, as close as they had been in his childhood. Dressed in black, and wearing as always her white organdie widow's cap with streamers, sitting up with her back ramrod straight, Maggie had a smile on her face.

'I'm sure that we can manage for the time being, Louis. You're putting on weight and writing an essay a month for Scribner's, as well as getting on with your new novel. What more could you ask for?'

'I confess that I'm more productive at present than I've ever been before. There may be many reasons for that. I don't think that I'm unduly mercenary – I certainly don't spend a lot of time calculating my income and expenditure – but I can tell you that the seven hundred pounds a year that I get from Scribner's for producing one essay a month actually amounts to more than I earned during the whole of the previous five years. Financial security settles anxiety and boosts industry. And yet there are times when I feel guilty at accepting so much money, especially as I'm now a man of independent means.'

'This is America, Stevenson,' I told him, with a note of impatience in my voice. 'You're simply being paid at a commercial rate. The publishers know full well that, since the success of *Jekyll and Hyde*, your work will sell, and earn them a handsome profit.'

By that stage, the name of R.L. Stevenson was probably more famous in America than in England. When Louis had arrived in New York, he was besieged by reporters, and accommodated in one of the city's top hotels as the guest of a millionaire. It was a far cry from his first journey to the USA when he'd disembarked as an itching, scratching unknown.

'Yes, I confess that I enjoyed all the attention that the press gave me this time. I wallowed in the sensation of celebrity. When I was in England, I looked upon myself more as a literary type: worthy but obscure.'

Maggie laughed, a high-pitched happy laugh. 'Hardly obscure, Louis, when *Jekyll and Hyde* was the subject of sermons throughout the land. Whenever I heard your book being referred to from the pulpit, I felt so proud of you that I wanted to stand up and proclaim myself as your mother before the congregation. A mother's pride in her son, completely lacking in jealousy, is a joyous thing.'

As for myself, I have no direct knowledge of a mother's pride. My parents were divorced during my infancy, and I was brought up by grandparents in Paris. I didn't return to my birthplace, New York, until after the end of the Civil War. My mother has visited me at Saranac Lake on one occasion, and one occasion only. In other words, some of us have to get on in life without the encouragement of a proud mother.

'And how is Louis, doctor?' asked Maggie, as if she had arrived that day from the other side of the world.

'He's as well as you see him, Mrs. Stevenson,' I replied. I had not needed to take much medical interest in my famous patient. 'My visits to him are mainly for the purpose of friendly conversation.'

'Which is much appreciated, Trudeau. My conversations

with the other residents tend to be limited to the weather, hunting and fishing: subjects not necessarily close to my heart. I need a scientist to dispute with, even though your medical skills can be kept in reserve for the time being, from my point of view.'

'Are his lungs in good shape, Dr. Trudeau?' asked Maggie. 'He hasn't had a single cold since he came here, and no blood spitting. Mind you, we're following Fanny's rule that no-one with a cold should be admitted to the house; even Lloyd has been banished to the village hotel for a few days until his nose is clean.'

My face, already red from the heat of the fire, hid my embarrassment. Surely my own cold was no reason to curtail visits, or to take time off my duties. I have never allowed trivial ailments to interfere with my work; the fight against consumption is too important for that.

'I'm glad to say that I can't find any signs of lung disease. We must call it arrested consumption.'

'Fanny would be pleased to hear you use the word consumption.' Louis's shoulders sagged as he spoke. 'It's so much more romantic than catarrh, bronchitis or bronchi-whatever.'

I was taken aback by his reaction. A diagnosis of consumption is usually made, or at least assumed, long before a patient reaches Saranac Lake. 'Well, Stevenson, it's true that we have no proof of tuberculosis in your case, even using the most up to date scientific methods. Bronchiectasis – damage to the airways by repeated infection in childhood – could explain your history, including all those serious haemorrhages. It's difficult or impossible to be sure about this, on the basis of the evidence that we have at our disposal.'

Maggie looked doubtful. 'Louis has been so very ill so many times. Does consumption always mean tuberculosis?'

'Consumption means tuberculosis of the lungs, no more and no less,' I replied. 'Sometimes the disease can become arrested, and therefore difficult to diagnose but, thanks to modern bacteriological methods, we're making great strides in our understanding of the condition. Nevertheless, we can't see into the lungs and, even if we could, the answer wouldn't necessarily be obvious.'

Louis had left his seat and was standing leaning against the end of the mantelpiece, which was corrugated by a series of burns produced by cigarette ends. I knew from Andrew Baker that Stevenson's bedding had also become the victim of his smoking habit: sheets perforated by circular burns, blankets permeated with the clinging smell of tobacco.

Not for the first time, I found myself staring at Louis's face, as I tried to analyse the fascination of the luminous eyes, set so peculiarly far apart, and the mellifluously attractive speech. It was not the words themselves that impressed me but the way they were spoken, with confidence, and at the same time with vulnerability. The 'gifted boy' was nearly the same age as myself, and yet there were times when he evoked in me paternal feelings of protectiveness.

'It's not for me to understand the mysteries of modern medicine.' Louis jabbed the air with his cigarette. 'I'm simply a writer struggling to produce my daily quota of words on a page. And, in Saranac Lake, that's not as straightforward a task as you might think; for example, frozen ink creates a certain practical difficulty. Perhaps I should follow Lloyd's example and clatter away at a typewriter. What do you think, Trudeau?'

'I don't have any views on that matter, Stevenson. On another front, though, I would dearly like you to understand what we're trying to do here at Saranac Lake to conquer tuberculosis once and for all. Please, let me show you my laboratory. I may not be able to explain to you the mysteries of modern medicine but I think that I can give you a vision of the future.'

Louis grimaced. 'I hardly dare look into the future. The future is not my territory.'

Nevertheless, it was agreed that he would have a conducted tour of my laboratory at the earliest opportunity.

Chapter Sixteen

IN THOSE DAYS, the laboratory was no more than twelve feet long and eight feet wide, a tiny wing of a big house. My wife, my son, my daughter, my baby son, they needed the expanse of the house. Myself, I needed the privacy of the laboratory, where I could enter another world, a world of hope and discovery, far removed from the daily round of sickness and despair. Looking down my microscope, focusing on the minutiae that could lead me to a bigger picture, I was oblivious to everything outside. It was as if all the mental energy from my years of enforced inactivity had been stored up and was now available for release as an intense beam, illuminating microscopic clues to the cause and treatment of disease. At the age of 39, I had the heart and mind of a young scientist, uninhibited by the experience and disillusion usually associated with the descent into middle age.

There was scarcely enough space for Louis to squeeze into the laboratory beside me. A good part of the room, under a small window, was taken up by a table, on which a microscope, slides and bottles of stains were aligned. Next to this was a bucket containing the water supply and, beyond that, a discoloured sink, drained by a lead pipe into a battered waste pail.

The grey light of the winter day seeped in through the window, partly obscured by powdery snow, drifting gently on the ledge and from time to time blowing across the panes of glass. Standing opposite Louis, I looked him in the eye. I felt in this place, on my own territory, a calm self-confidence. It seemed that my authority over him was emphasised by my starched white jacket, buttoned all the way up to protect my shirt from the splash of stains.

'Let me start at the beginning. On this shelf, always kept on top of all other books and papers, is the most valuable Christmas present that I've ever been given in my life. It's a translation of the paper published in 1882 by the German scientist, Robert Koch, who proved beyond doubt that tuberculosis is caused by a micro-organism, the tubercle bacillus. A momentous publication. A perfect example of scientific logic. I can tell you, Stevenson, that my first reading of this paper produced in me a feeling of intense excitement, which is difficult to explain and impossible to exaggerate.'

'I think I know what you mean, Trudeau. Rather like one's first reading of a poem by Walt Whitman, perhaps.'

I looked at Louis's face, his brilliant eyes, his gentle smile, and I was uncertain of the meaning of this remark. Was it serious? I smiled back at him, a rather fierce grin probably, and I continued my discourse, as if I was talking to an errant but favourite pupil.

'I'm not talking about poetry, Stevenson, I'm talking about the use of scientific method to prove the cause of a disease which kills one seventh of humanity on the face of this earth. As soon as I read Koch's paper, I realised that, if I could learn to stain and recognise the tubercle bacillus under the microscope, then I would be able to identify the micro-organism in the spit of my consumptive patients, thus proving the diagnosis of tuberculosis. But – and this is far more important – I also realised that, if I could learn to grow the micro-organism on a culture medium outside of the body, and then inoculate this into guinea-pigs, then I would be able to produce tuberculosis at will!'

'Hold on. Let me get this straight in my mind. Are you saying that you want your animals to suffer from tuberculosis?'

I smiled again, exhaling noisily and impatiently. I clenched
my fists in front of me to emphasise what I was trying to
explain. 'Yes, and no. You're missing the point. If it's possible to
produce tuberculosis in guinea-pigs or rabbits, then we can
experiment with substances that might kill the bacillus in the living animal. I'm talking about the possibility of chemicals curing
tuberculosis. And if we can find a substance that does this, then
we can eliminate the disease from the world.'

'A noble aim indeed, considering that we're talking about a
disease dating back to the beginning of civilisation, and which
our old friend Hippocrates seemed to understand as well as
many modern physicians.'

'Hippocrates didn't understand the cause of consumption,
Stevenson: it was Koch who discovered this, and we've known
it for only five years. Now sit at the table here and look down
the microscope at that slide. I want you to see the little devils.'

Louis looked down the barrel of the microscope with his
right eye, whilst I adjusted its mirror to reflect daylight from the
window up through the slide.

'Use the wheel to focus the microscope, Stevenson, and
you'll see a vague background. Now focus more carefully and
you'll see a scattering of bright red-coloured rods standing out
against the background. Those red rods are tubercle bacilli,
micro-organisms which are the very cause of the disease.'

'I think I can see a few red marks which look as though
they've been made by careless strokes of a paintbrush. They
don't look particularly devilish.'

'Oh yes they are. Each of those little rods is only three or four thousandths of a millimetre long, but together they add up to a formidable army of invasion. Imagine the surge of happiness that I felt when I first successfully showed them up on a slide, after months of fruitless attempts, attempts which led to more staining of my clothes and shoes than of the slides themselves. It was with a sense of wonder that I first gazed at those little red rods, and then a sense of anger, a desire to join battle with them. Can you understand that, Stevenson?'

'I think so,' he replied, still twiddling with the focusing wheel, trying to get a clear view of the enemy. 'You're angry with the disease, but surely not with these little red paintbrush marks.'

'It's the other way round. I can acquiesce in the disease process as it affects myself – and it's no secret that I first came to the Adirondacks because of my consumptive state – but I cannot allow the bacilli which are the cause of this world-wide plague to go unchallenged.'

'I'm sure that Fanny would love to hear such fighting talk. She's never recovered – never will recover – from the death of her little son Hervey. It's over ten years since he died of consumption, but I swear that Fanny thinks of him every day, and probably every night as well. She has some kind of mission to fight the disease.'

'Good for her. Never disparage her for that. And believe me when I tell you that I can understand how she feels.'

I wasn't exaggerating when I said this. Over twenty years earlier, when I was only 17 years of age, I had looked after my brother during his death from consumption. And I really did look after him. We slept in the same room – the same bed in fact – I fed him and I bathed him, I even carried him up and down the stairs. I did everything for him. As for the doctor, he gave us a bottle of cough medicine and told us that the window should never be opened. Whatever you do, he said, you must keep out the cold air.

'Stevenson, it was the death of my own brother from consumption that determined the direction of my life, which is now more than ever devoted to waging war on the disease.'

I was aware of shakiness in my speech, trembling hands, a hint of tears. After all, my energy and capacity for work were self-generated, and the strength of my views was untempered by contact with professional colleagues. I didn't publish a medical paper until I was 37; even then, I was so nervous at the prospect of presenting it to a medical meeting in Baltimore that I fainted – yes, I fainted, flat out – on the platform. My authority in Saranac Lake was derived from belief in myself. I had no need of stimulus and criticism from others.

Louis gazed at me, as if trying to comprehend the depth of my feeling. 'And would your brother have survived with modern methods of diagnosis and treatment?' he asked.

'Perhaps not,' I replied. 'He had rapidly progressive, galloping consumption. But his last days would have been more comfortable here than in a New York garret. Why should the best treatment be available only to the wealthy? I intend to build up a sanatorium here that can be used by any who suffer from consumption, regardless of how much they happen to own in the way of worldly goods. That's why I'm raising subscriptions from the rich, Stevenson: it's to pay for the poor. The first cottage of the sanatorium – we call it the Little Red – was opened just two or three years ago, and we're still charging just five dollars a week, making up the rest of the cost from our general fund. This means that the poor, as well as wealthy people like you, can take advantage of the Adirondacks. At the same time I can study their disease process, and so advance my understanding of it. You see how it all hangs together, Stevenson.'

'I can only say that if my father had been a poor man, then there's no doubt that I would have died years ago. It seems to me that I've spent most of my adult life in search of health. Yes, I can see what you're getting at, Trudeau.'

'Well then, let me take you on to the next step: growing the tubercle bacillus outside of the body.'

I showed him some glass tubes containing blood serum on which I'd planted tubercle bacilli from the glands of a diseased guinea-pig. The organisms had grown – in other words, multiplied – on the serum after three weeks in my home-made thermostat. They could be seen under the microscope.

'The first time that I achieved success with this procedure was the happiest moment of my life, a moment of pure joy, undiluted by any feeling of anxiety. It was like a fairy tale come true. You see, Stevenson, once I'd produced a culture of the bacilli in the laboratory, I could use this at will for my experiments with guinea-pigs and rabbits.'

Louis was beginning to look doubtful. 'Just a minute, you've lost me. Where does the blood come from?'

'Oh, I bought a sheep for three and a half dollars, and then I sacrificed it. I needed only one animal: it provided more than enough blood for my research.'

'My dear Trudeau, I have a vision of you as Abraham in the land of Moriah, slaying a beast in place of the beloved son.'

'You've got a strange way of looking at things. The sacrifice of the sheep was necessary in the cause of science, which will benefit all of us.'

'Except the sheep, perhaps.'

'Only that particular sheep.' I took off my pince-nez and slowly polished the lenses. It was important that I should maintain my composure. 'Now in this box on the corner of the bench, you will see one of my guinea-pigs. They don't actually live in the laboratory, because it's much too cold for them during the night. Their home is a kind of underground cellar, dug out by myself and kept comfortably warm by a modern kerosene lamp. They live in their boxes on a system of shelves in the cellar, as cosy as can be.'

Louis peered into the box at the small animal, with its rat like face and whiskers. His friendly gaze was not returned by the guinea-pig, which was intent on nibbling at some milk-soaked bread. 'Not a pretty beast, really, but no doubt you could learn to love him.'

'Stevenson, you must remember that I'm a scientist, and also a hunter. I can't afford the luxury of sentimentality for animals. My guinea-pigs are the key to a cure for tuberculosis. Once I have inoculated them with tubercle bacilli, then I can experiment with chemicals that might kill the bacilli within the living animal. And if we can find such a chemical, then we can cure tuberculosis in humans. You see the beauty of it?'

'Beauty is not the word that I would use. But tell me, have you had any success with your chemicals?'

'No, not so far. Remember that I'm still at an early stage of experimentation. I've injected animals with substances such as creosote and carbolic acid. Unfortunately, the tubercle bacillus was more resistant to these chemicals than were the animals themselves – or late animals, perhaps I should say.'

Louis paled. He sat down. The faintest of shudders passed through his body. 'Is all of this necessary, Trudeau?'

'Yes, yes and yes again. We must press on until we have the answer.'

Carefully, I explained that my research had already proved, with certainty, the benefit of a favourable environment. Experiments had shown that tuberculous rabbits allowed to run wild in the fresh air were less likely to die than those kept in crowded conditions.

'In other words, if you have tuberculosis, then a good climate – such as we have in the Adirondacks – will undoubtedly prolong your survival.'

'I thought we already knew that.'

'We might have known it, but that's not the same as proving it. Koch has shown us that it is only the application of scientific method that will lead to real advances in medicine. This is the light of the future.'

Louis backed towards the door of the laboratory, his right hand held up in front of him, almost as if he wanted to push me away.

'Trudeau, your light may be very bright to you, but to me it smells of oil like the devil!'

The wooden door creaked to a gentle close. Gentle, but it was a dramatic exit. I knew that Louis had recently completed an essay entitled 'The Lantern Bearers', and I could only assume that the story-line was still colouring his imagination. My attempt to involve him in the excitement of scientific discovery had failed, utterly failed. Surely it is self-evident that the study of disease holds out the only real hope of relief for humanity from sickness and suffering, and what brighter light can there be than that? I have never noticed the 'smell of oil'. During the time that I knew Louis, I respected his literary gifts, of course, but I was always worried by his tendency to retreat into a land of make-believe. The sad truth is that the cruelty of the real, grown-up world can be conquered only by direct confrontation.

I sat at the table and stared through the window, watching Louis as, hands thrust deep in the pockets of his overcoat, he plodded along the snow covered path on his way back to Baker's Cottage. Bewildered by this man, I reflected that we are sometimes more astonished by events which don't occur than by those which actually happen. Throughout our discussion of modern ideas on the cause of tuberculosis, Louis had failed to ask the obvious question: had tubercle bacilli been found in the laboratory examination of his own spit? As a matter of fact, the answer to this question was no. For all my talk of possible 'arrested' disease, I was well aware that Louis might never have had tuberculosis; the more mundane diagnosis of bronchiectasis could explain everything in his medical history. In my view, it was a distinction hardly worth making. The famous author was staying at Saranac Lake, and his health was in better order than it had been for years. Surely that was good enough for both of us.

Chapter Seventeen

MY VISITS TO BAKER'S COTTAGE continued much as before. There was no rancour in Louis's attitude, and indeed no indication that a dispute between us had ever occurred. Early in March of 1888 the *New York Evening Post* published a letter from the famous author, extolling the virtues of the 'Adirondack Cottages for the Treatment of Pulmonary Disease', and signalling that there was a need for funds from the rich and generous. He even included my figures for the number of patients cured or improved during their stay – I reckoned this to be 40 out of 51 during the previous year – and he referred to the 'physician of the establishment' by name. I couldn't have imagined a better advertisement for Saranac Lake. Of course it was also an advertisement for myself. That is much the same thing. I accept that the name of Trudeau must be used to 'personalise' fund raising. Anyone who knows me will tell you that I abhor any idea of wealth for myself, but at the same time I do need a flow of donations to maintain the quality and reputation of the sanatorium.

The figures quoted in Louis's letter for patients cured or improved were impressive. Not surprisingly, our good results were resented in some quarters. From time to time I was accused by various sceptics of selecting for treatment only those mild cases who would improve wherever they were. I had to force myself to ignore such cynical criticism, knowing that there would be no purpose in accepting patients with advanced disease, and also knowing that success, especially by a lone practitioner, will always provoke jealousy. The fact remains that I, Edward Livingston Trudeau, a man forced by ill health to drop out of his hospital career at an early age, became within 15 years a pioneer of sanatorium treatment for tuberculosis. In 1888, I was a scientist ahead of my time. And I had achieved this by my own efforts without the benefit of professional patronage, except for patronage meaning condescension. I have never allowed my work to be undermined by unfair criticism and general tittle-tattle.

I enjoyed my visits to Baker's Cottage, arguing with Louis in a friendly way on all manner of subjects. Of course I was aware that he would have preferred an adversary with a more significant knowledge of literature than I possessed, but at least we could discuss politics and the philosophy of science. One thing that we did share was a dislike of the social graces. I shall never forget the occasion when Louis shut the door firmly behind some well-dressed visitors with the words: 'Trudeau, it is not the great unwashed whom I dread; it is the great washed'. It was a remark that cemented a kind of friendship between us.

Towards the end of March, I found myself sitting by the log fire in Baker's Cottage, not with Louis (who was closeted with his pen and ink) but with Fanny and Lloyd. Fanny had returned to the Adirondacks during the previous month, feeling unwell in a non-specific and rather mysterious way. It was apparent that the Stevensons' time at Saranac Lake would soon come to an end.

'Louis has recovered completely from the influenza that hit him last month, doctor. He became unwell after I returned, but you can be sure it wasn't me who infected him. My illness was altogether different. And it wasn't me who produced an outside temperature of 40 degrees below zero at night. Is this climate really good for him?'

'Undoubtedly it is, Mrs. Stevenson. He was unfortunate in catching influenza from your maid, but he's recovered, and without any blood spitting. That must be something of a record for him. And he's actually put on weight during the winter. Not a bad result for Saranac Lake!'

Fanny, sitting close to the fire, with her hands outstretched as near to the flames as the heat would allow, looked sideways at me. Her gaze – unwavering, unblinking – fixed my own, less certain, returning stare with an irresistible intensity. 'We've had enough of Saranac Lake, Dr. Trudeau. We only intended to come for a few months, and that was as a substitute for Colorado. Louis accepts that cold weather and high altitude are bad for my health. He needs me – I'm sure you know that – but I just can't cope with the climate up here. We're thinking of moving off within a few weeks.'

'Louis is never better than when he's at sea.' Lloyd jumped up to speak, gesticulating in a way that seemed to imitate Louis's manner. 'We've spent many happy evenings during the winter making imaginary plans for yacht trips, perhaps in the Indian Ocean, perhaps the Pacific, perhaps the Atlantic. It all started as a kind of game, but Louis now says that fantasy may become reality. It's all wonderfully exciting.'

My impression was that Lloyd took himself too seriously for a 19-year-old, but perhaps it was just his appearance. A good six feet tall, he held his head back a little. His half-closed eyes looked at me through oval spectacle lenses, a special pair in a lightweight frame ordered from New York.

'Lloyd is collaborating with Louis to produce a new story.

What better apprenticeship could there be than that for an aspiring writer? Tell the doctor about it, Lloyd.' Fanny spoke eagerly, proud of her handsome son.

'It's a comedy centred on a wrongly identified corpse and a disappearing coffin.' He was talking about *The Wrong Box*. 'Louis will tell you that it's mainly my work, but of course his suggestions and amendments have been invaluable. The only sad thing is that I haven't converted him to the use of the typewriter.'

Fanny reached up to take her son's hand and pulled him down to sit close beside her. 'You forget that Louis is nearly twenty years older than you are. He's not at an age when men change their methods of work just because a new invention has come along. It's you who represent the future.'

'Maybe,' replied Lloyd, 'but it was Louis who bought the typewriter for me in the first place. His mind isn't closed to new ideas: our collaboration has shown that. He likes the comradeship of our work, the joy of being together and exchanging ideas. He wants the lines that he's written to win the approval of someone whose opinion he values. At the same time, I need his guidance and his encouragement for my own work. It's a two way process.'

Lloyd's thin-framed spectacles gradually slipped down the bridge of his nose as he spoke, so that he had to incline his head further and further back to look through the lenses. His prominent, almost Roman, nose gave him a patrician air that made me feel, in a peculiar way, uncultured. For a brief moment, I was irritated to realise that I would have valued his approval.

Fanny was still holding Lloyd tightly to her side. 'Collaboration or no collaboration, we simply must uproot ourselves within the next few weeks. I'm going to California soon, Dr.

Trudeau, to meet my daughter Belle – she's nearly 30 now, with a son of her own – and maybe I'll find somewhere for us to stay during the summer.'

'Make it a yacht, Mother, make it a yacht. Louis says that we can afford it, using his inheritance. Too much money at his disposal confuses him. He wants to put it to good use: he wants to spend it. And Aunt Maggie is keen to go with us.'

'We need whatever is best for Louis's health,' replied Fanny, 'and we have Dr. Trudeau to thank for looking after him during the winter. No one can deny that Saranac Lake is a first rate place for treating consumption.'

'Very few of my calls on your husband have been professional,' I admitted. 'The fact of the matter is that he's been well throughout most of the winter, thanks to the climate of the Adirondacks no doubt rather than to myself. In any case, he doesn't altogether approve of my laboratory work, you know.'

Fanny gave a brief, low-pitched laugh. 'Oh, I know about that. You must forgive him. He prefers not to be reminded of the unpleasant facts of life, and he has no feel for anything practical or experimental. He couldn't repair a door handle or hang a picture on the wall without my help. Surprising really for someone who once studied engineering, although his heart was never in that, you know. And as far as doctoring is concerned, I think he'd prefer all his physicians to be versions of Sir Andrew Clark: never upsetting, always reassuring.' She looked steadily at me, her mouth smiling with a hint of mischief.

'That's all very well,' I replied, tersely, 'but conservatism doesn't bring about any advance in medical science. We have to do more than reassure our patients.'

I couldn't bring myself to make polite noises about Sir

Andrew Clark, aware as I was of his stubborn reluctance to accept the bacillary theory of tuberculosis. His dismissive comment that 'the bacillary hypothesis, although supreme in the domain of pathology, continues to be of but small account, or even barren, in the field of practical medicine' remains to this day stuck in my memory as a symbol of outdated attitudes; and this was a statement published in 1885, fully three years after Koch's discovery! The ornate, tortuous style of Clark's writings, blessedly few in number, belongs to a past age, which can have no relevance to the approaching dawn of the twentieth century, a century during which the power of science will surely carry the day.

She seemed to understand my point of view. 'I like to keep up with advances in medicine, Dr. Trudeau. That's why I subscribe to *The Lancet*. I owe it to Louis to keep an eye out for any promising new treatment.'

'In that case,' I replied, deliberately sidestepping any discussion of Louis's diagnosis as such, 'you'll appreciate that modern bacteriological methods offer the best hope of conquering tuberculosis.' I emphasised the word 'conquering'. Yes, I believe that we are engaged in something like a military campaign. Perhaps I'm too much the son of my father, who fought as an officer for the Southern Army during the Civil War, and then returned to work as a doctor in New Orleans, eventually neglecting his practice in favour of hunting. But I'm not a man to abandon my profession or family. In any case, I never knew my father, who walked out on us when I was an infant. It's all fruitless speculation. And yet I wish that we could have met. I'd like to have a clear image of him in my mind.

She looked doubtful. 'I suppose that I appreciate the promise of modern bacteriology.'

She had learnt from her reading that the death rate from tuberculosis in Britain was falling year by year. 'That can't be put down to the promise of new methods of treatment, can it?'

'Well,' I replied, 'during the last 30 years or so we've had the advent of sanatorium treatment, the realisation that climate has an important influence.'

'Helpful to the rich, no doubt. What about all the ordinary people? They don't get sanatorium treatment.'

'Maybe they don't, but generally better, less crowded, housing must have reduced the risk of transmission of tubercle bacilli from person to person. It stands to reason that this would be so.'

Fanny took this to mean that the declining death rate from tuberculosis had come about as a result of improvements in social conditions, which started long before the discovery of the tubercle bacillus.

I hesitated, aware that I was losing the argument to a person of untrained but superior intelligence. 'Mrs. Stevenson, I only say that if by scientific method we can find a substance which kills tubercle bacilli without harming the human body, then we can eradicate tuberculosis from the face of the earth.'

'There could be no greater blessing for mankind than that. If only I could have given my little Hervey a substance which killed the disease and left him unharmed. He would be 16 now, and a young man of great artistic talent. I've no doubt about that, no doubt at all. Instead of which his bones lie in a grave at St. Germain. That's right, isn't it Lloyd?' She spoke in a low voice, almost inaudible.

'Yes, that's right Mother,' replied Lloyd. 'You see, Dr. Trudeau, we could afford only a temporary resting-place for

Hervey at St. Germain. After ten years his bones were to be transferred to a common grave. Anyway, that hasn't happened. Louis has sent money to ensure that it will never happen. He knows how important this is to my mother.'

Although tempted to talk of my own loss, the brother whose death had steered me into a medical career, I decided against this luxury, knowing from experience that patients and their relatives rarely show any interest in their doctor's sensibilities. Fanny had burdens enough of her own without needing to hear about mine.

'In any event, Dr. Trudeau, we all know that you're doing good work, and you're certainly putting Saranac Lake on the map. When I arrived here, it was by horse and buggy for the last 20 miles. Now we have a railroad all the way to the village. That's a tribute to your fame.'

I waved a hand dismissively, but I was pleased by the compliment. I was beginning to make my mark on the world, and a railroad all the way to my sanatorium was a pretty good sign of this. Saranac Lake was indeed 'on the map' and, for many people, the name was synonymous with that of Edward Livingston Trudeau.

'I'll miss my conversations with your husband more than I can say, Mrs. Stevenson. Any dispute between us has been essentially good natured, thanks to the generosity of his spirit. I'm not exactly a literary person, but I shall join the queue to buy any book that he cares to publish in the future. And may there be many of them.'

* * * * *

Soon after Louis left Saranac Lake in April 1888, he sent along a set of half a dozen of his books, specially bound for presentation to me. In each volume was inscribed a verse of dedication to a member of the Trudeau family. In *Dr. Jekyll and Mr. Hyde* he wrote:

Trudeau was all the winter at my side:
I never spied the nose of Mr. Hyde.

Part Five:
Dr. Bernard Funk's Narrative

Chapter Eighteen

SAMOA HAS BEEN MY home since February 1880. I came here from Hamburg with a contract to work as medical officer for the German firm that owns the big plantation on the island of Upolu. It is this plantation – coconut, pineapple, coffee and cacao – which for many years has given the firm its stranglehold on Samoan trade. We have a workforce of over eight hundred 'blackbirded' (imported, mainly kidnapped) men and women, plus native Samoans and German managers. Naturally, my professional services are directed predominantly towards my fellow Germans, most of whom live at the western end of Apia, which is the port and capital of the island. But I act also as private practitioner to the British and American communities on the eastern side of the town. For a long time I was Upolu's only doctor, except for surgeons from visiting warships. This has invested me with self-confidence, to some degree. A man in single-handed medical practice on a South Pacific island must be guided by his knowledge, his conscience, his textbooks and the Almighty. There are no 'second opinions'. And, in addition to his professional work, a doctor on Upolu must take care to maintain an awareness of shifting political allegiances, so complex on an island with three great powers involved in government, entwined with many strands of native Samoan rivalries. Looking back at that month of September, 1892, I recall that it was not the easiest time for relations between Robert Louis Stevenson and myself. During the two years that Louis had lived on Upolu, he had involved himself too heavily in local politics, championing a Samoan faction and irritating the British Consul by writing long letters to *The Times*, using his name as a famous author to advance contentious political opinions. It was said that the Consul was involved in a plot to get Louis deported from the island. Certainly such a move would have had widespread support within the German community. Many of us still believe that the Stevenson influence on Samoa worked against our national interest.

This was a difficult situation for me but, as I have explained, I was at that time the only doctor on the island, and therefore it was generally accepted by my compatriots that I could and should visit Louis whenever this was needed for professional reasons. In any case, the Stevensons were always welcomed at any Apia social function that they cared to attend. On such occasions, German and Anglo-Saxon rivalries were submerged in the general currency of gossip.

It was a nuisance to me that Louis lived three miles inland from Apia, six hundred feet above sea level at Vailima, where the author's isolated house had been built soon after his arrival on the island. There was a good road for the first mile out of Apia but then for the next two miles just a track. It was rough riding, and quite unsuitable for a carriage or even a buggy. A visit to Louis was an expedition, taking up a whole morning or a whole afternoon.

On this particular day, late in September, I was summoned to Vailima by Maggie. She told me, curtly, that it had taken her more than two hours to locate me, and that she didn't particularly enjoy riding through the streets of Apia looking for a doctor. Instantly recognisable by her white widow's cap and jet-black dress flowing down to her ankles, she was an incongruous sight on the island. In my view, she didn't carry enough authority to summon me at a moment's notice. Surely she must have known that my main duty was to the German firm, not to the Vailima household. I have always made a point of ensuring that I can be found in or around Apia within a few hours. In my experience, such a delay is rarely if ever harmful to a patient, and often quite helpful to the process of diagnosis. For years, the British here have complained about the arrogant behaviour of the Germans towards them, but really it's the other way round. Despite my command of the English language, I have always found my British patients less amenable and less willing to follow advice than my fellow-countrymen.

And so it was at a leisurely pace that I rode alongside the couch grass lawn in front of Louis's house at Vailima. A spacious two-storey building, painted peacock blue, with verandahs at both levels and a red corrugated iron roof. To the west, densely forested green slopes rising to the peak of Mount Vaea, thirteen hundred feet above sea level, gently dominated the Stevenson acres below. It was an estate suitable for a man of means.

Tethering my horse at the back of the house, I waved at Fanny, busy tending her kitchen garden. An energetic figure, wearing blue overalls, and with dishevelled grey curly hair escaping chaotically from underneath a wide-brimmed soft hat, she continued digging at speed, attacking the ground, muttering at it. She didn't see me, or perhaps chose not to acknowledge my arrival. I unclamped the cigar from my jaws and I shouted – a stentorian voice, impossible to ignore – 'Good day to you, Mrs. Stevenson'. She looked at me for a moment, half waved, and then resumed her fierce forking of the soil.

Beyond the kitchen garden stretched the Stevenson plantation, mainly pineapple and cacoa, worked by a band of Samoan
labourers, with Lloyd as their overseer. Despite the appearance
of industry, I doubt that profit, or even self-sufficiency, was
achieved at Vailima. The household made good use of the Apia
shops, and the Stevensons were reputed to be overgenerous to
their servants.

Louis's room was on the first floor, at the corner of the
verandah. It was not Fanny and it was not her daughter Belle
who escorted me. It was Sosimo, Louis's Samoan manservant, an
important member of the house staff, a man devoted to his master,
who was known to them as 'Tusitala', the teller of tales. I followed
Sosimo's gleaming brown legs, his bare feet padding softly up
the stairs, leading me to my patient.

'Stevenson, your mother tells me that you're ill. We must
sort you out.' My considerable bulk took up too much space in
this small room, and the sound of my voice – loud, cheerful,
authoritative – seemed to bounce back at me from the walls. I
exhaled a generous cloud of cigar smoke, which engulfed the
thin ribbon trailing from the end of Louis's cigarette.

The narrow bed with its single blanket was unoccupied. He
was sitting at the table, dressed in white shirt and trousers – no
shoes – sorting out papers in a desultory way.

'My mother worries about me, Funk. She always fears that
a slight fever will progress to something worse. Sometimes she's
right.'

I stuck a thermometer under Louis's tongue. I tugged
thoughtfully at my beard (pointed and indisputably greying),
and then drummed with my fingers on the yellowed deal table
for a minute or two before unceremoniously pulling out the

thermometer. I glanced at the scale. 'Normal, my dear fellow, absolutely normal. How very encouraging.'

'Exhaustion, plain and simple, is my problem, Funk. I've finally reached the end of *David Balfour*, my new novel, and now I can allow myself to feel tired. My first significant female character – Catriona – and this is over 25 years from the beginning of my writing career. You can understand the effort that was needed! I've been working every morning from six o'clock, or even earlier than that, and some afternoons as well. Not just the novel, but my letter writing as well, not to mention my *Footnote to History*.'

I winced at the mention of Louis's Samoan history. It was rumoured that this would displease the German community, and indeed the British establishment. Why couldn't he spend his time writing another *Treasure Island* instead of dabbling in politics? Leave politics to the politicians, I say.

I walked over to the open window at the front of the room and leaned out. It was the dry season, and the temperature must have been near to 90 degrees Fahrenheit, but there was moisture in the air, a hint of recent showers. Far below, the sea sparkled into the distance, a myriad of dazzling points reflecting the sunlight. The depth of the silence was broken only by the faint, regular boom of the surf. Unusually for me, I said nothing. I had no wish to engage in a debate on Samoan history.

'I'll tell you this, Funk: I've done more work in Samoa than I've ever done before. In two years, I've had a sore throat once, and influenza once, but nothing serious, no blood spitting. And I've been more active physically than ever before, weeding the garden and riding my pony. Of course, I was ill when I went to Australia early last year, but fever always strikes me in Sydney.

You don't need to be a medical genius to realise that it's the Samoan climate that protects me from illness. That's why I'm staying put.'

Louis had spent two years cruising the South Seas in search of health before he settled here. 'I was well at sea – only one illness with blood spitting – but I was sick at Tahiti and sick at Sydney with the heaviest of colds. Samoa has saved my life.'

I was thirsty, devilish thirsty. I wanted to drink a bottle of beer quickly, or possibly a glass or two of the dry Monopole champagne that Louis had shipped in. I've never been able to understand why my patients assume that I don't want to drink when I'm on duty. This is Upolu. I'm always on duty, and it should be obvious that I need a drink from time to time.

'Your health is excellent, Stevenson. No more needs to be said about it. The problem, put simply, is that you work too hard. As far as I can see, you're supporting your mother, your wife, your stepson Lloyd, your stepdaughter Belle, her husband and child, not to mention at least a dozen servants and some of their wives – and now your cousin Graham as well. You're a patriarch of the old school.'

'I hardly think so.' Louis paced the confined space of the room with a skill that must have come from much practice. A thin cigarette burned slowly between the fingers of his left hand. His hair was short and greying. He looked older than his 41 years. 'It's true that this place is infernally expensive to run, and I'm earning more than five thousand pounds a year from my books, but my mother is going to help out with the cost of the extension that we're planning – it was her idea in the first place – and Belle has been paying her way as my amanuensis since I developed writer's cramp.'

I hope that I suppressed the guffaw that I felt erupting inside me. There was a rumour in Apia that the swarthy Belle was the illegitimate daughter of Stevenson by a Moorish woman, and another rumour that Louis had started the rumour himself. Others nodded and winked at the amount of time that Belle spent in Louis's company, taking notes to his dictation, squeezing out his reliance on Fanny. Belle's husband Joe – banished to the beach in a haze of alcohol, dishonesty and adultery – was no longer an impediment, they said, and nor was their son Austin, who had recently been sent to school in California at Louis's expense. Such was the swirl of Apia gossip concerning the Stevenson household. It was deliciously interesting at times but not to be mistaken for the truth. My own natural tendency to spread gossip is inhibited, I am glad to say, by my profession.

I was anxious to leave for Apia. Louis's company, his conversation, was always attractive, even when he was at his most introspective, but I needed beer and food. That was the main thing. Sweating, mopping my face with a large crimson handkerchief, I stood and picked up my black bag, to signal my imminent departure.

'I must leave you to your books, Stevenson.' The wall shelves were filled with bound volumes – brown, red, blue and green, with gold lettering on the spines, all varnished for protection from damp – arranged and disarranged, apparently at random. 'And don't forget to leave a decent pause between each cigarette.'

'I've a grand memory for forgetting, doctor.'

I laughed out loud, a neighing, echoing laugh. Perhaps this was one of Louis's quotable remarks which Cusack-Smith, the British Consul, reckoned were delivered to all guests as a means of self-advertisement. On the other hand, I must record that

Cusack-Smith's limited sense of humour was submerged under a swamp of envy. He was jealous of Louis's political influence.

Fanny, picking her way across the garden, was ready to speak to me as I was on my way out. 'Is it serious, doctor?'

'No, no, Mrs. Stevenson. It's just brain-fag. He's been over-working, as I'm sure you know. His health is basically sound.' I beamed at her, and then slowly drew on my cigar, uncertain how she would react to my reassuring words.

'I suppose so.' She frowned, and looked away from me. 'When we came to Samoa, I expected to spend most of my time looking after Louis, nursing him and helping him with his writing. And yet, as things have turned out, that's not been needed. Anyway, with all these servants, work doesn't mean work, it means supervision. Except for my garden, of course. I spend hours out here, digging, weeding, planting. I love my garden, but then of course I would. Louis mocks me as a peasant. I know my place.'

'A peasant? That remark was meant as a compliment, Mrs. Stevenson. You can be sure of that.'

'I wish that I could,' she replied, 'but I'm happy enough out here. Let Belle and Louis spend their time closeted indoors, if that's what they want to do. I need fresh air, and plenty of it. There's nothing else that will settle my pounding headaches. Uncle George told me years ago that I must have an aneurysm in my head. He recommended chlorodyne. I recommend fresh air.'

'I agree with you, dear lady.' On more than one occasion I have been accused of being opinionated, but I would never be arrogant enough to pretend that I could recognise cerebral aneurysm on the basis of a history of headaches. Any doctor

worth his salt will tell you that it is impossible to make the diagnosis before fatal rupture of the aneurysm has occurred. It's a
post-mortem diagnosis. The professors who taught me in Berlin
would not have let 'Uncle George' get away with such an unsub-
stantiated statement, based no doubt on his assessment of what
Fanny wanted to hear. She had medical licence to refer to her
headaches as 'my aneurysm', the words somehow imbuing her
condition with a mysterious danger, more frightening to others
than to herself.

She held the horse's reins as I heaved myself up on to the sad-
dle. Even that brief effort took my breath away, and made my
heart pound protestingly in its cage. Fresh beads of sweat sprung
out on my face. I needed refreshment. And anyway my body,
misshapenly rotund, was not designed for physical exertion.

I took the reins from her hands, so endearingly small and
roughened: the hands of a worker, with more interest in service
to others than pride in herself.

'Take care as you ride home, Dr. Funk. We shall need you
again.'

Chapter Nineteen

JANUARY – THE MIDDLE OF the rainy season in Samoa – was actually a month of brilliant sunshine in 1894. Each day the sun rose in a cloudless sky, and the house at Vailima shimmered, floated, in a sea of green. By noon, without even a hint of breeze, the verandahs were uncomfortably hot, but the great hall, which occupied the entire ground floor of the extension to the house, was perceptibly cooler, its light and heat dimmed by the varnished Californian redwood of the walls and ceiling.

I sat at the plain dining table, with my chair pushed well back to accommodate my girth. Fanny, wearing her blue overalls despite the heat of the day, sat at the head of the table, her fingers idly exploring the grain of the wood. Her right leg, crossed over her left knee, swung to and fro with an irregular, impatient rhythm. Louis was apart, perched on a bench under the window, getting up every so often to walk up and down, or round the table, as he talked. His tanned, ruddy face looked good and healthy against the whiteness of his shirt. His long, narrow, bare feet were brown and weather hardened. Louis and Fanny smoked, consumed, a succession of their thin-rolled cigarettes, whilst I enjoyed a large, slow-burning, eminently chewable, cigar. But there was only a faint tobacco fug in the air of this extravagantly spacious room.

'It's a pleasant task for a doctor to visit healthy patients,' I boomed. 'What a pity that your mother isn't here to compliment me on my good work.'

Louis grinned, apparently understanding the hurt feeling, as well as the humour, behind my remark. It was nearly a year since Maggie had departed for Scotland. In fact it was almost time for her return. Believing, as she did, that I had treated her family in a cavalier manner, she had left me with the threat that she would come back with a young doctor. A joke no doubt, but barbed. She disconcerted me, perhaps even frightened me a little, even when she was on the other side of the world. When Louis caught influenza (a disease that periodically sweeps over this island with devastating effect), it was impossible for me to attend him, but I took the precaution of sending a deputy, the doctor from a German man-of-war. In this way, I was able to establish that the episode of blood spitting was brief and relatively mild. After that, there was only one other period of haemorrhage – in August – and I can say without fear of contradiction that this was the result of an ill-advised, over-vigorous game of lawn tennis. Admittedly, he was ill again in October – feverish on a visit to Hawaii – but otherwise remarkably well. A pretty good health record for a year in the life of an invalid! Maggie would have no grounds for criticising me.

I think that Louis agreed with me about this. 'I confess to being well, and working for as many hours in the day as I've ever done. And yet I can wake up, quite suddenly, in the blackest of moods, unable to distinguish why I feel that way, struggling in the dark to get some perception of the cause of it.'

'Why struggle?' I replied. 'It's enough to be alive with a good appetite and a good thirst. Speaking as a man who's seen death at close quarters when I served as a surgeon in the Franco-Prussian war, I can tell you that life is too short for soul-searching.

I learnt that lesson again when my house was full of wounded and dying during the rebellion last July.'

Louis's oval face was, for once, impassive. And, because this was so unusual, his very impassivity seemed to signal an emotional response to my remark. I really shouldn't have brought up the subject of the Samoan war in which Mataafa, the rebel chief supported by Louis, was defeated. There was gossip in Apia that Louis was involved in Mataafa's military planning, but you can discount such stories. Louis was a dreamer, not a man of action. Characteristically, he picked the losing side. The German community forgave him for this and took some pleasure from it. Of course his status in the eyes of Mataafa's Samoans was greatly enhanced.

'That's exactly what I've been telling Louis, doctor. Just go from day to day. His health has never been better and, in any case, he's always got me to rescue him whenever needed. It didn't take me long to rush over to Hawaii in October and get him better again. If you ask me, Louis's work will be my memorial as well as his.' Fanny spoke with confidence, even some aggression. I was amazed at her resilience. Only eight or nine months earlier, her family had feared that she was close to death: she wouldn't leave her bed, wouldn't speak, wouldn't eat. I had been worried about her as well but I knew that it was not a physical illness. She had slipped into a state of depression, acquiescing in it, not using her natural belligerence to resist it. She had retreated into herself and had lost contact with those around her. It was a situation that was not suited to my habit of giving brisk, optimistic directions. Nevertheless, I had called in at the home regularly, repeatedly reassuring a distraught Louis that she would survive. And indeed she did survive, gradually resuming her usual daily activities as if nothing untoward had happened. Her recovery was complete within a few months, and was reinforced by her rescue of Louis from his illness in Hawaii. Belle might be his amanuensis and literary confidante, but it was still Fanny who was needed in a crisis.

'You're absolutely right, Fanny. Without your help I would've been dead years ago. But I can't live just one day at a time. I have to search my experience and motives in order to grind out my books, and that can be a painful process, sometimes too painful to sustain.' Louis revealed that he'd set aside *Weir of Hermiston*, his book exploring the relationship between father and son. 'It's seven years since my father died, and yet, strangely, he's in my thoughts more and more each day. I think of him as a young man and myself as a small boy. I think of us on holiday. I see him running along the sands and splashing into the sea. I yearn to speak to him and touch him again. His influence over me is stronger now than at any time since I was a child. It's difficult to understand, and even more difficult to explain.'

Louis was speaking to us but he wasn't looking at us. Standing in the far corner of the room, he was studying the portrait that hung in a prominent position over the piano: his father, painted by Sir George Reid.

Fanny got up, walked slowly towards her husband, linked arms with him, and then led him to the table to sit with us. 'The old man would be proud of you now, Louis. If only he could be here to see you as the respected head of this household. If only he could see you presiding each week over the Vailima prayers: you, the son that he feared was doomed to lifelong atheism. And if only he could see that you've succeeded as a writer beyond your wildest dreams, with an income way beyond anything you could have earned as an engineer. I know that he would be proud of you.'

'Perhaps so,' replied Louis, dragging on his cigarette, and still gazing across the room at the portrait.

Suddenly, lost in the hinterland of my own thoughts, I burst out laughing. 'My father always said that I was a lazy devil. And he was right. That's why I've ended up in Samoa, thank God, well away from the rigours of the fatherland.'

'Louis is here for the sake of his health, Dr. Funk.' Fanny fixed me with a steady, unblinking gaze. It was the gaze of my first schoolmistress, who would pull my hair mercilessly whenever I made a stupid comment. I looked away in some discomfort.

'Of course, of course,' I replied. 'Your health is excellent, Stevenson, unlike our Samoan friends whose heads were chopped off in the war. And unlike poor Isla Sitwell, come to that.' My tongue, loosened by a couple of glasses of Louis's beer, was beginning to gabble. I knew it, but that doesn't mean I could stop it.

Louis inclined his head to one side. His eyes glistened. 'I suppose you're saying that there can be no hope for Isla. He was in Samoa for such a short time, and yet long enough to win our hearts with his gentle, innocent nature, more like a child than a young man. He reminded me so much of his cousin Bertie, who was just 18 when he died in Davos all those years ago: the same spiritual calm, the same bodily fragility.'

'Stevenson, you must be realistic. There can be no doubt that the young man has consumption. I found the tubercle bacillus in his spit, and that proves it, beyond argument. You were right to send him away. We have enough experience of consumption amongst the natives of this island to know that the climate would soon have finished him off. Believe me, he needs the cold, dry air of the mountains if there is to be any chance of recovery.'

'If you say so.' Fanny's American accent, not usually noticeable to me, became more obvious when she was angry. 'But surely even you will admit, Dr. Funk, that the climate here has done wonders for Louis's health.'

'My professional calls have been mercifully few,' I replied. Despite the comfortable warmth of the alcohol in my blood, I managed to restrain myself from saying anything further. Visitors, friends and relatives might assume that Louis had tuberculosis – his thin frame, his bright eyes, his well known history of fever and blood spitting – but in reality there was nothing to confirm this. And if he did have tuberculosis, with those symptoms, over so many years, then why did he appear to be well when he was in Samoa? To my mind, it is more likely that Louis suffered from that condition which goes by the unglamourous and unmemorable name of bronchiectasis, a disease which can persist for many years and yet allow a reasonably active life. After all, bronchiectasis is characterised by repeated lung infection and haemorrhage. In Louis's case, these episodes seemed to be ignited by colds, and the fewer colds that he had – either at sea, or in the pleasantly warm climate of Samoa – the less likely was any period of serious illness. Sometimes, indiscreetly perhaps, I would attempt to explain this to friends of Louis, using words more familiar than bronchiectasis, such as asthma or bronchitis. I admit that this may have led to confusion. But I never attempted to explain my opinion in Fanny's presence. She believed in Louis as a consumptive, an artist who must continually fight against the burden of disease and who could achieve nothing without her strength to sustain him. There was no purpose in arguing about the matter with her. In any case, I was never really interested in discussing the minutiae of diagnostics with anyone. I am essentially a surgeon: my attention is more likely to be captured by a severed limb than by a cough. And as for Louis, he showed no curiosity about the cause of his illness, simply relief at periods of well-being.

'Certainly Samoa is good for my health. A man can't complain when he outlives his doctor. There must always be an element of satisfaction in that.' Louis looked across at me. 'Of course, I'm not referring to your good self, my dear Funk,' he added.

It was Fanny who explained this. 'Sir Andrew Clark is dead. Not a physician necessarily known to yourself, Dr. Funk, but a great man in his own country. It was a strange experience for us to follow the course of his fatal illness, with the news delayed by the month or more that it takes for the mail to reach us from London. Each time that Louis emptied the big waterproof bag of letters and papers brought up from the mail steamer, I took out my copies of *The Lancet* and hurriedly looked for the latest news, unable to suppress my sense of foreboding, despite knowing that the printed page was weeks out of date. Sir Andrew was working as usual when he was struck down, in his study, the very room where Louis and I saw him all those years ago. It was a stroke, paralysing the right side of his body and taking away his speech, that wonderful rich speech which, over the years, had given strength to so many of his fellow human beings. He never left that room: he was attended there by a nurse sent from The London Hospital and, nearly three weeks later, he died there. On one day, over six hundred people, the poor as well as the wealthy, called at the house to ask about his condition. He was a famous man, and much loved. Mr. Gladstone was one of the pallbearers at the funeral, and crowds lined the route all the way from Westminster Abbey to Kings Cross, where there was a special train waiting to take his body to the little churchyard near his country house in Hertfordshire. He was a physician of great distinction, Dr. Funk.'

'I can't say that I've ever heard of him,' I replied. 'Was he a man to rival Koch?'

'I don't think that he wrote much, and I'm pretty sure that he never discovered anything new. He was too busy looking after his patients. That's how he made his name, and that's how he made his fortune. He left over £200,000 in his will.' Fanny managed to sound both admiring and critical at the same time.

'Imagine that, Funk.' Louis gripped me by the elbow with his long, bony fingers and gave me a friendly shake. 'Two hundred thousand jingling quid! I thought I was well off when we sold our house in Bournemouth for £1,500, but he could have bought us out a hundred times over and still have had a fortune left in the bank. Mind you, a few of his guineas came from me, or perhaps I should say from my father, but I got my money's worth. He seemed to understand me, and I really do believe that he cared for me. Of course, he wouldn't have had time to spend all the money he was earning. I suspect that he died of overwork, and nothing would have pleased him more than that. But what a funeral! I doubt that mine will rival that.'

'How can you know that?' asked Fanny. 'Perhaps twenty years hence you'll be a wealthy baronet. In any case, your name will live with your writing and will still be known the world over in a hundred years' time. Dr. Clark's fame will die with his patients.'

Inappropriately perhaps, I hooted with laughter. 'For some of us, avoiding infamy is enough of a struggle without bothering to seek fame. I thank God that I was never cursed with ambition.' I puffed on my cigar and blew a cloud of smoke up towards the ceiling. I slurped beer, happily spilling a thin stream of it over the expanse of my comfortable, cream coloured waistcoat. Life in Samoa was good.

'And as for you, Stevenson, you are in the prime of your life: 43 years old, and with your health in better shape than it's ever been. So let there be no further talk of funerals.'

Chapter Twenty

ALTHOUGH I CANNOT KNOW how many more years of life the Lord will grant me, I am certain that, however much may seep from my memory, I will still recall the events of Monday the 3rd of December 1894 with precise, slow-paced, accuracy.

I was at home – my house is at the western end of Apia Bay – and it was not long after six o'clock in the evening. As usual at this hour, I was preparing to mix cocktails, a process that customarily takes me at least ten minutes, calculating and measuring out the constituents with delicious anticipation. The announcement that Lloyd was at the door upset me. A call from the Stevenson household would inevitably mean a journey out to Vailima. Whatever was wrong – whether it was with Louis, Fanny or Maggie – was certain to be regarded by them as something requiring my immediate presence. I knew that I wouldn't run the risk of incurring Maggie's pointed displeasure or Louis's gentle rebuke. I would have to abandon my cocktails.

There was a sense of urgency, panic even, about Lloyd that was all the more powerful for being totally out of character. I was more accustomed to his languid manner: the local patrician who was more English than the English, the man who didn't care to be seen hurrying, the man who had travelled the world. It was my belief that, if the whole of Apia were to go up in flames, Lloyd would stand by and say: 'Oh yes, I've seen this sort of thing before'.

Thus it was with astonishment that I found myself being driven at high speed towards Vailima. Lloyd had commandeered the horse and buggy, having given his own pony to Anderson and told him to ride post-haste to the Stevenson house. In some ways it was a relief that Anderson – the surgeon from HMS *Wallaroo*, the British warship harboured at Apia – would be there first. Perhaps he would sort things out, or at least deal with any immediate crisis. On the other hand, the *Wallaroo* had been in port for only a few weeks, not enough time for Anderson to get to know the Stevensons. The Royal Navy surgeon was an unknown quantity.

What could be wrong? I turned it over in my mind. Louis had 'collapsed'. Lloyd hadn't witnessed this, but had been told by a breathless and frightened Belle to get the doctor as soon as it was humanly possible to do so. 'Collapse' could mean anything, or nothing. Louis had been well for months – he hadn't even had a cold since June – and working for as many hours in the day as he had ever done. Why should he have collapsed? Perhaps he did have tuberculosis after all. Perhaps he'd developed a pneumothorax, the sudden deflation of a diseased lung with air escaping inside the chest cavity. In that case, I might need to insert a drain into the chest. And yet how could I do that without any equipment to hand? No, impossible: Louis didn't have tuberculosis – that was a romantic fantasy – he had bronchiectasis. I told myself to calm down and think straight. Perhaps the 'collapse' was something completely new, possibly a convulsion, in which case he might well have recovered by the time we reached the house. That would make everything easy. I was beginning to wish that I'd swallowed a couple of cocktails before setting off from Apia, and indeed I would have done so if Lloyd hadn't been standing over me. Despite my need for alcohol, I knew that the sight of a drink going into my mouth at speed would not have inspired confidence in my ability to deal with a crisis. I folded my arms, and I pressed them together to control the insistent trembling of my sweaty hands.

The horse and buggy careered along the road to Vailima, jolting so roughly that I feared I would be thrown off at any moment. Darkness was falling by the time we reached the final stretch, a wide grassy track cut through dense foliage. High up above us, silhouetted against the evening sky, the huge fringed leaves of coconut palms swayed in the breeze. This was 'The Road of the Loving Heart', which had been laid by Mataafa's Samoans and opened with due ceremony less than two months earlier: a gift to Louis in recognition of all the help that he'd given to the rebels during their period of imprisonment.

The house came into view with the ground floor windows, illuminated by the oil-lamps inside, cut out of the darkness. As I stared at the rectangles of light, wondering what was going on inside, Samoan boys, chattering and shouting, came running with lanterns to guide us. And when at last we reached the front of the house, and the horse was tethered, I stepped out of the buggy and strode across the verandah into the hall, my apprehension and shakiness suppressed by an ingrained habit of appearing (and, strange as it may seem, feeling) calm at that critical point when action is needed.

Louis was semi-recumbent in the big green leather armchair. It was his grandfather's chair, which had been shipped in from Edinburgh and brought up to the house by bullock and cart only six months earlier, with the local transport arrangements in the hands of the German firm (the same firm that was derided by the British amongst themselves but used whenever they needed help with a difficult job of work).

Fanny and Maggie were kneeling, one on either side of Louis, rubbing Louis's feet, sponging them gently with hot water. The *Wallaroo* doctor was busying himself ordering the boys to open windows. The cool night air, with its heavy fragrance of gardenia, sharpened and sweetened the oil-lamp fustiness of the room. Belle – tense, involved – was helping with the windows. All were occupied save Louis, his eyes wide open but with no sign of awareness.

Fanny moved aside as I curled my fingers at Louis's wrist and felt the pulse over a full minute, timing it with my pocket watch, giving myself a space to observe and to think. Just 50 beats to the minute, the pulse was slow and absolutely regular, like the tolling of a funeral bell.

After the minute had ended, I held on to his wrist and, turning towards Fanny, I asked her to tell me what had happened.

'It was so quick,' she replied. 'He was as well as ever earlier on, dictating *Weir of Hermiston* to Belle. He was happy. He fetched a bottle of Burgundy up to go with our dinner. Then he came to help me as I was preparing a salad. That was when it happened. He was standing by my side, at the table on the verandah at the back of the house. He was right next to me, adding oil to my mayonnaise mixture. He was almost touching me. And then he suddenly fell to his knees and propped himself against the table. 'What's that?' he said, with his hands held to his head – 'Do I look strange?' Sosimo and I carried him in here and put him in the armchair. Within a few minutes – maybe less than that – he lost all consciousness. He hasn't spoken a word since then. He doesn't even seem to recognise us. What is it that's wrong with him, doctor? Please tell us.'

Louis's eyes stared, unseeing, at the ceiling, his pupils, each a wide pool of darkness, surrounded by a thin rim of brown iris: dead, fish eyes, no longer the gems that had sparkled just an hour earlier. His breathing stopped,all was quiet, and then resumed, breaths deeper and deeper and then gradually fading, quiet again until, just when all seemed lost, a faint gasping restarted and gradually built up, the desperate cycle repeating itself.

I pulled up the front of Louis's jumper, a sailor's jumper, and pushed a thermometer into his armpit. As I waited, I was hit by a wave of sadness which rushed through me and then, racing away, left me with the sure knowledge that I was looking at that thin and feeble chest for the last time. I leaned over him and listened with my stethoscope to the periodic breathing, but in my mind it was the sound of Louis's voice again: 'I want to die with my clothes on.' After this, I pulled out the thermometer, held it up to the light of the overhanging oil-lamp, and – with a hand now as steady as could be – I rolled it between thumb and forefinger until the scale came into view. 95 degrees Fahrenheit. An ominously low temperature.

I straightened up and, with my face set in a way that could give no hope, looked across Louis at Maggie. She returned my gaze and then lowered her eyes. In that moment I saw that she understood and accepted everything.

It was time to confer with my colleague. I walked over to Anderson, who was still standing on the sidelines, and we went into a professional huddle, whispering to each other, with our backs to the Stevenson family.

'Well?' I asked him.

The young naval surgeon, his face reddening by the second, spoke quickly, the words stumbling over each other. 'I've made a mistake, such a foolish mistake. It was when I arrived, when I examined him – I'd never clapped eyes on him before – I was so astonished by the thinness of his arms, I just blurted out 'how can anybody write books with arms like these?' His mother got upset. She rounded on me. What an idiot I am.'

Nothing is more reassuring to a man of mature years than a mistake by a younger colleague. Well used to making blundering remarks myself, I put my hand on his shoulder. 'Don't worry, it's not the first time she's rounded on a doctor.'

We whispered further, and then returned to Maggie and Fanny. After a moment's hesitation, I told them. 'It's an apoplectic stroke. I'm very sorry. There's nothing further that we can do.'

Nothing further to be done in that sense, but we had to fill time. I ordered the Samoan boys to bring a bed into the hall, to give Louis a resting-place more dignified than the armchair. This they did – it was a sturdy brass bedstead – and then four of them slowly carried him over to it. With exquisite care, and in silence, they laid him on the bed, and there he looked more peaceful, and ready for prayers to be said over him.

I went out on to the front verandah. I would have to stay, I would have to make sure that what I had said was correct. I am not by nature a humble man, but I freely admit that patients have been known to recover unexpectedly after being pronounced beyond hope by myself. Having implied that Louis's death was imminent, I prayed that events would take their course sooner rather than later, for the sake of all concerned. And I needed a smoke to soothe me. It was not likely that anybody would offer me a drink, but I judged that no one would begrudge me my cigar.

Leaning on the rail of the verandah, I found that I was trembling again. Suddenly aware that I was participating in a momentous event, I wished that I could be elsewhere. Perhaps I would be blamed for Louis's death, although in reality there was nothing that I could have done to anticipate this catastrophe. It was ironic that Louis, who had survived profuse haemorrhages from his lungs, should succumb to a haemorrhage into his brain, a haemorrhage probably so small that it that it might not even fill a thimble, but within the brain large enough to destroy life. Nothing could have predicted or prevented this. The lifelong sufferer from lung disease, the well-known consumptive who never had consumption, was confounding his doctors to the last.

It was not so very long before I was called back into the great hall. Maggie was kneeling in prayer. Gently lifting Louis's wrist, I felt for the pulse that wasn't there. I waited for the next breath that would never come. I pulled out my pocket watch and flicked open the cover. It was ten past eight.

The next day, forty Samoan men hacked out a path from Vailima up to the top of Mount Vaea, long ago chosen by Louis as his burial-place. The funeral took place that very afternoon. I wasn't there. It would have been impossible for me to undertake such a steep climb even if I'd been invited to attend. Friends in Apia wondered why the funeral hadn't been held in town; it could have been one of the grandest occasions in the history of Samoa. As for myself, I was surprised and disconcerted to realise that I felt a raw sense of loss, the loss of a brother. And I knew then that the name of Funk would be remembered in future years simply because of my presence at Vailima on one day, Monday the 3rd of December 1894.

Notes, Acknowledgements and Sources

The Strange Case of R.L. Stevenson is fictional, but it rests on a foundation of factual material.

For much of the detail concerning RLS's life, I consulted the biographies, especially *The Life of Robert Louis Stevenson* by Graham Balfour (Methuen & Co., 1901), *The Life of Robert Louis Stevenson* by Rosaline Masson (W. & R. Chambers, 1923), *Voyage to Windward* by J.C. Furnas (Faber & Faber, 1952), *Robert Louis Stevenson* by James Pope Hennessy (Jonathan Cape, 1974), *RLS A Life Study* by Jenni Calder (Hamish Hamilton, 1980) and *Robert Louis Stevenson* by Frank McLynn (Hutchinson, 1993). *I Can Remember Robert Louis Stevenson*, edited by Rosaline Masson (W. & R. Chambers, 1922) provided a wealth of information on RLS's personal characteristics.

The Letters of Robert Louis Stevenson, edited by Bradford A. Booth and Ernest Mehew (Yale University Press, 1994-1995: 8 volumes) was my invaluable guide for the time sequence of events, and showed me the way to many other sources of information. I am grateful to Rebecca Thurgur of Yale University Press (London office) for her help.

I derived and extrapolated RLS's views from his letters, essays and works of fiction, and incorporated some of his words into the narratives.

For further detail on the life of Fanny Stevenson I consulted *The Violent Friend* by Margaret Mackay (Doubleday & Co.,

1968) and *Fanny Stevenson* by Alexandra Lapierre (Fourth Estate, 1995), an exhilarating biography giving deep insight into Fanny's personality.

Dr. Andrew Clark's Narrative
(Chapters One to Seven)

Sir Andrew Clark (1826-1893), born in Aberdeen, was one of the most prominent of late nineteenth century London physicians. He received a baronetcy in 1883, and was President of the Royal College of Physicians of London from 1888 until his death.

For details of Clark's life, I consulted *Life of Sir Andrew Clark* by W.H. Allchin (1896), an unpublished manuscript (with associated documents) held by the Library of the Royal College of Physicians of London. I am grateful to the College for permission to use information derived from the manuscript (MS-15), and to quote (on pages 31 and 41) from the associated document Private Practice (MS 711/46): 'Temporary general directions', and 'Directions for managing an incipient feverish cold'.

Clark's Lumleian lectures on some points in the natural history of primitive dry pleurisies (published in the *British Medical Journal*, April 1885) described some of his views on bronchiectasis. I found further details of his life and work in the extensive obituaries published by the *British Medical Journal* and *The Lancet* (1893). I referred to *The London, A Study in the Voluntary Hospital System* by A.E. Clark-Kennedy (Pitman Medical Publishing Co., 1963) for the history of The London Hospital in the nineteenth century.

I obtained most of the information about RLS's childhood

illnesses from reading his mother's diary notes, as published in Volume 26 of the Vailima edition of *The Works of Robert Louis Stevenson*, edited by Lloyd Osbourne and Fanny Stevenson (Wm. Heinemann, 1923). The diary also refers to the meeting of the Stevenson parents with Clark in November 1873.

RLS saw Clark in London in October 1880, as indicated in Balfour's biography. I couldn't find any reference (in this or other sources) to Fanny accompanying her husband on his visit to Cavendish Square. In writing Chapters Five to Seven, however, I made the assumption that she was present at the consultation, so that I could speculate on her interaction with Clark.

Background information on Fanny's experiences in Antwerp and Paris (in Chapter Five) and in California (in Chapter Six) was derived from the biographies by Margaret Mackay and Alexandra Lapierre – particularly the latter, with its informative quotations from Fanny's letters.

In Chapter Six, RLS's account of his transatlantic voyage was adapted from his description in *The Amateur Emigrant* (1895).

Dr. Karl Ruedi's Narrative
(Chapters Eight to Ten)

Dr. Karl Ruedi was born near Chur, in the Rhine Valley. After spending his early professional years in Colorado, he worked in Davos from 1875 to 1891. He then achieved his ambition of returning to Colorado, but the venture was unsuccessful. His final years were spent at Arosa (near Davos), where he died in 1901.

My main sources of information on the medical aspects of

Davos were: 'On Davos as a Health Resort' by Clifford Allbutt (*The Lancet*, October 1877), *Davos Platz and the Effects of High Altitude on Phthisis* by Alfred Wise (J. & A. Churchill, 1881) and *Influence of Climate in Pulmonary Consumption* by Charles Theodore Williams (Smith, Elder & Co., 1877).

For social and weather conditions at Davos in 1880-1882 I relied on *The 'J.E.M.' Guide to Davos-Platz* by J.E. Muddock (1890) and *Robert Louis Stevenson at Davos* by W.G. Lockett (Hurst & Blackett, 1934). Lockett's interesting book also provided much information on RLS's family life at the resort.

In Chapter Eight, RLS's complaints to Ruedi about the Davos landscape and its psychological effects were adapted from descriptions given in his 'Swiss Notes', as published in *Essays of Travel* (Chatto & Windus, 1905). His account of tobogganing was derived from the same source. I obtained information on the writing of *Treasure Island* from RLS's 'My First Book: Treasure Island' (first published in *The Idler*, August 1894).

Dr. Thomas Bodley Scott's Narrative
(Chapters Eleven to Fourteen)

Dr. Thomas Bodley Scott (1851-1924) was a much loved General Practitioner who later became Mayor of Bournemouth. I obtained details of his life story from the short memoir *Thomas Bodley Scott Mayor of Bournemouth* (Ernest Cooper, 1924); I am grateful to Bournemouth Reference Library for access to this book, and to Bodley Scott's *The Road to a Healthy Old Age* (Fisher Unwin, 1917). For more information on Bournemouth medical practice in the 1880s, I referred to *The Medical Aspects of Bournemouth* by Horace Dobell (Smith, Elder & Co., 1885).

For background information on the 'Skerryvore' household, I used *RLS and his Sine Qua Non* by Adelaide Boodle (John Murray, 1926), and 'RLS at Skerryvore' by William Archer (first published in *Critic*, November 1887).

In Chapter Fourteen, RLS's account of the dream relating to his father was adapted from 'A Chapter on Dreams' (first published in *Scribner's Magazine*, January 1888), which was also a source of information on the dream underlying *Strange Case of Dr. Jekyll and Mr. Hyde*.

At the end of Chapter Fourteen, I have quoted RLS's Dedication to *Underwoods* (Chatto & Windus, 1887) in full.

Dr. E.L. Trudeau's Narrative (Chapters Fifteen to Seventeen)

Dr. E.L. Trudeau (1848-1915), for many years a world authority on pulmonary tuberculosis, was founder and director of the Saranac Lake Sanatorium (this was known in his day as a 'sanitarium' but, to avoid confusion, I have used throughout the more generally accepted word 'sanatorium'). Following the discovery of X-rays by the German scientist Roentgen in 1895 (the year after RLS's death), Trudeau established a Chest X-ray unit at the sanatorium. Effective drug treatment for tuberculosis (Trudeau's aim) did not begin until 1944, when Waksman discovered streptomycin; unfortunately, the subsequent decline in tuberculosis has in recent years been partly reversed by the development of drug-resistant disease. The modern-day Trudeau Institute is an independent, non-profit making, biomedical research institute with a staff of over 100, working mainly in immunology, including a programme aimed at combating the rising incidence of tuberculosis.

For details of his life and work, I relied heavily on *An Autobigraphy* by E.L. Trudeau (Lea & Febiger, 1916), a frank and moving account of his fight against disease. I adapted Trudeau's words to explain some aspects of his early life and career in Chapters Fifteen to Seventeen, and also his explanation to RLS of laboratory work in Chapter Sixteen.

In Chapter Fifteen, RLS's explanation to Trudeau of the origins of *The Master of Ballantrae* was derived from 'The Genesis of The Master of Ballantrae' (Edinburgh Edition of Stevenson's Works, Volume 21, 1896).

Dr. Bernard Funk's Narrative (Chapters Eighteen to Twenty)

Dr. Bernard Funk was born in Mecklenburg, Germany. He studied medicine in Berlin and then served as an Army surgeon in the Franco-Prussian war of 1870-71. After working for a time for the Hamburg-American Steamship Company, he entered into an engagement with Messrs. Godeffroy & Son, a German firm with large interests in Samoa. He emigrated from Hamburg to Samoa in 1879. In addition to his work for the German firm and in private practice, he was Samoa's Health Officer until his retirement in 1904. There is a photograph and short biography of him in *The Cyclopedia of Samoa* (McCarron Stewart, 1907), and I am grateful to the Apia Public Library for providing a copy of this.

My main sources of information on the Vailima household were: Balfour's biography of RLS, Margaret Stevenson's *Letters from Samoa* edited by Marie Clothilde Balfour (Methuen & Co., 1906), Fanny and R.L. Stevenson's *Our Samoan Adventure* edited by Charles Neider (Weidenfeld & Nicolson, 1956) and

Memories of Vailima by Isobel Strong and Lloyd Osbourne (Archibald Constable & Co., 1903).

Details of Stevenson's death were derived mainly from Booth and Mehew's *The Letters of Robert Louis Stevenson* Volume 8, Epilogue (Belle Strong's Journal, plus letters written by Lloyd Osbourne and Fanny Stevenson).

* * * * *

Finally, I am grateful for help received from the staff of the following libraries: National Library of Scotland; The British Library; Leeds University Health Sciences Library; Leeds University Brotherton Library; the Library of the Royal College of Physicians of London; Wellcome Institute Library, London; British Medical Association Library, London; Bournemouth Reference Library; Bradford City Libraries; Nelson Memorial Public Library, Apia, Samoa.

A Chronology of R.L. Stevenson

1850   Born at 8 Howard Place, Edinburgh, on 13 November
1853   Family moves to 1 Inverleith Terrace, Edinburgh
1857   Family moves to 17 Heriot Row, Edinburgh
1861   Enters Edinburgh Academy
1863   Visits France (Menton), Italy, Austria and Germany
        with parents
1864   Enters Mr. Thomson's private school (for delicate and
        backward boys) in Frederick Street, Edinburgh
1865   Educated by private tutors
1866   *The Pentland Rising* printed privately at father's
        expense
1867   Enters Edinburgh University
1870   Visits Earraid islet (off the Ross of Mull) during the
        construction of the Dhu Heartach lighthouse
1871   Quits study of engineering and starts law classes
1872   Formation of the L.J.R. (Liberty, Justice and
        Reverence) club
1873   Meets Mrs. Sitwell during a visit to Suffolk
        First consultation with Dr. Andrew Clark
        Travels to the south of France
        Essay 'Roads' published in *Portfolio*
1874   Returns to Edinburgh
        'Ordered South' published in *Macmillan's Magazine*
1875   Called to the Scottish Bar
1876   Walking tour of Carrick and Galloway
        Canoe trip in Belgium and France with Walter
        Simpson

Meets Fanny Osbourne at Grez-sur-Loing
1878 'Crabbed Age and Youth' published in *Cornhill Magazine*
An Inland Voyage published
Fanny returns to California
Walking tour with a donkey in the Cévennes
1879 *Travels with a Donkey in the Cévennes* published
Journey to California
Fanny obtains divorce from Sam Osbourne
1880 Marries Fanny in San Francisco
Silverado honeymoon
Returns (with Fanny and Lloyd) to Scotland
Journey to Davos
1881 Swiss Notes published as essays in the *Pall Mall Gazette*
Virginibus Puerisque published
Returns to Scotland and starts work on *Treasure Island* at Braemar
Second winter in Davos
Treasure Island serialised in *Young Folks*
Visit to Berne (during Fanny's illness)
1882 *Familiar Studies of Men and Books* published
Leaves Davos
New Arabian Nights published
Moves to the south of France
First performance of the play *Deacon Brodie* (in Bradford)
1883 Takes up residence in Hyéres
Black Arrow serialized in *Young Folks*
Treasure Island published as a book
The Silverado Squatters published

1884   Moves to Bournemouth, living at first in a boarding house and then in rented accommodation (Bonallie Towers)

1885   *A Child's Garden of Verses* published
Moves to 'Skerryvore', Alum Chine Road, Bournemouth
More New Arabian Nights: The Dynamiter published
Visit to Dorchester and Exeter
Prince Otto published

1886   *Strange Case of Dr. Jekyll and Mr. Hyde* published
Visit with father to Smedley's Hydropathic, Matlock Bridge
Kidnapped published
Holiday in Paris

1887   *The Merry Men and Other Tales* published
Death of Thomas Stevenson in Edinburgh, on 8 May
Tribute to father 'Thomas Stevenson: Civil Engineer' published in *Contemporary Review*
Leaves for America with his mother, Fanny and Lloyd
Underwoods published
Settles at Saranac Lake for the winter
Memories and Portraits published

1888   'A Chapter on Dreams' published in *Scribner's Magazine*
'The Lantern-Bearers' published in *Scribner's Magazine*
Leaves Saranac Lake for New York and then California
Black Arrow published as a book
Voyage on the yacht *Casco* to the Marquesas, the Paumotus Islands and Tahiti

1889   Arrives in Hawaii

The Wrong Box published
Voyage on the schooner *Equator* to the Gilbert Islands and Samoa
The Master of Ballantrae published

1890 Buys land on Upolu, Samoa
Sails on *SS Lübeck* to Sydney
Voyage on the trading steamer *Janet Nicholl* in the South Seas
Returns to Upolu to live at Vailima
In the South Seas published

1891 Another trip to Sydney

1892 *Across the Plains* published
The Wrecker published
A Footnote to History published

1893 House extension at Vailima completed
Another trip to Sydney
Island Nights' Entertainments published
Samoan rebellion
Visit to Hawaii
Catriona published

1894 *The Ebb-Tide* published
The 'Road of the Loving Heart' built
44th birthday feast
Dies suddenly, on 3 December
Buried on Mount Vaea

1895 *The Amateur Emigrant* published

1896 *Weir of Hermiston* published

1897 *St. Ives* published

Some other books published by **LUATH** PRESS

FICTION

But n Ben A-Go-Go
Matthew Fitt
ISBN 0 946487 82 0   HBK   £10.99

The Bannockburn Years
William Scott
ISBN 0 946487 34 0   PBK   £7.95

The Great Melnikov
Hugh MacLachlan
ISBN 0 946487 42 1   PBK   £7.95

POETRY

Poems to be read aloud
Collected and with an introduction by
Tom Atkinson
ISBN 0 946487 00 6   PBK   £5.00

Scots Poems to be read aloud
Collected and with an introduction by
Stuart McHardy
ISBN 0 946487 81 2   PBK   £5.00

**Caledonian Cramboclink: verse,
broadsheets and in conversation**
William Neill
ISBN 0 946487 53 7   PBK   £8.99

Blind Harry's Wallace
William Hamilton of Gilbertfield
introduced by Elspeth King
ISBN 0 946487 43 X   HBK   £15.00
ISBN 0 946487 33 2   PBK   £8.99

Men & Beasts
Valerie Gillies amd Rebecca Marr
ISBN 0 946487 92 8   PBK   £15.00

The Luath Burns Companion
John Cairney
ISBN 1 84282 000 1   PBK   £10.00

'Nothing but Heather!'
Gerry Cambridge
ISBN 0 946487 49 9   PBK   £15.00

FOLKLORE

Scotland: Myth Legend & Folklore
Stuart McHardy
ISBN 0 946487 69 3   PBK   £7.99

**Luath Storyteller: Highland Myths
and Legends**
George W Macpherson
ISBN 1 84282 003 6   PBK   £5.00

The Supernatural Highlands
Francis Thompson
ISBN 0 946487 31 6   PBK   £8.99

Tall Tales from an Island
Peter Macnab
ISBN 0 946487 07 3   PBK   £8.99

Tales from the North Coast
Alan Temperley
ISBN 0 946487 18 9   PBK   £8.99

ON THE TRAIL OF

On the Trail of John Muir
Cherry Good
ISBN 0 946487 62 6   PBK   £7.99

**On the Trail of Mary Queen of
Scots**
J. Keith Cheetham
ISBN 0 946487 50 2   PBK   £7.99

On the Trail of William Wallace
David R. Ross
ISBN 0 946487 47 2   PBK   £7.99

On the Trail of Robert Burns
John Cairney
ISBN 0 946487 51 0   PBK   £7.99

**On the Trail of Bonnie Prince
Charlie**
David R. Ross
ISBN 0 946487 68 5   PBK   £7.99

**On the Trail of Queen Victoria in
the Highlands**
Ian R. Mitchell
ISBN 0 946487 79 0   PBK   £7.99

On the Trail of Robert the Bruce
David R. Ross
ISBN 0 946487 52 9   PBK   £7.99

On the Trail of Robert Service
GW Lockhart
ISBN 0 946487 24 3   PBK   £7.99

On the Trail of The Pilgrim Fathers
J Keith Cheetham
ISBN 0 946487 83 9 PBK £7.99

LUATH GUIDES TO SCOTLAND

Mull and Iona: Highways and Byways
Peter Macnab
ISBN 0 946487 58 8 PBK £4.95

South West Scotland
Tom Atkinson
ISBN 0 946487 04 9 PBK £4.95

The West Highlands: The Lonely Lands
Tom Atkinson
ISBN 0 946487 56 1 PBK £4.95

The Northern Highlands: The Empty Lands
Tom Atkinson
ISBN 0 946487 55 3 PBK £4.95

The North West Highlands: Roads to the Isles
Tom Atkinson
ISBN 0 946487 54 5 PBK £4.95

WALK WITH LUATH

Mountain Days & Bothy Nights
Dave Brown and Ian Mitchell
ISBN 0 946487 15 4 PBK £7.50

The Joy of Hillwalking
Ralph Storer
ISBN 0 946487 28 6 PBK £7.50

Scotland's Mountains before the Mountaineers
Ian Mitchell
ISBN 0 946487 39 1 PBK £9.99

LUATH WALKING GUIDES

Walks in the Cairngorms
Ernest Cross
ISBN 0 946487 09 X PBK £4.95

Short Walks in the Cairngorms
Ernest Cross
ISBN 0 946487 23 5 PBK £4.95

NATURAL SCOTLAND

Wildlife: Otters – On the Swirl of the Tide
Bridget MacCaskill
ISBN 0 946487 67 7 PBK £9.99

Wildlife: Foxes – The Blood is Wild
Bridget MacCaskill
ISBN 0 946487 71 5 PBK £9.99

Wild Scotland: The essential guide to finding the best of natural Scotland
James McCarthy
Photography by Laurie Campbell
ISBN 0 946487 37 5 PBK £7.50

Scotland Land and People An Inhabited Solitude
James McCarthy
ISBN 0 946487 57 X PBK £7.99

The Highland Geology Trail
John L Roberts
ISBN 0 946487 36 7 PBK £4.99

Rum: Nature's Island
Magnus Magnusson
ISBN 0 946487 32 4 PBK £7.95

Red Sky at Night
John Barrington
ISBN 0 946487 60 X PBK £8.99

Listen to the Trees
Don MacCaskill
ISBN 0 946487

CURRENT ISSUES

Trident on Trial
Angie Zelter
ISBN 1 84282 004 4 PBK £9.99

Some Assembly Required: behind the scenes at the rebirth of the Scottish Parliament
David Shepherd
ISBN 0 946487 84 7 PBK £7.99

**Scotland - Land and Power
the agenda for land reform**
Andy Wightman
ISBN 0 946487 70 7 PBK £5.00

**Notes from the North
Incorporating a Brief History of the
Scots and the English**
Emma Wood
ISBN 0 946487 46 4 PBK £8.99

HISTORY

**Reportage Scotland: History in the
Making**
Louise Yeoman
ISBN 0 946487 61 8 PBK £9.99

Old Scotland New Scotland
Jeff Fallow
ISBN 0 946487 40 5 PBK £6.99

Edinburgh's Historic Mile
Duncan Priddle
ISBN 0 946487 97 9 PBK £2.99

SOCIAL HISTORY

Shale Voices
Alistair Findlay
foreword by Tam Dalyell MP
ISBN 0 946487 63 4 PBK £10.99
ISBN 0 946487 78 2 HBK £17.99

Crofting Years
Francis Thompson
ISBN 0 946487 06 5 PBK £6.95

A Word for Scotland
Jack Campbell
foreword by Magnus Magnusson
ISBN 0 946487 48 0 PBK £12.99

BIOGRAPHY

**Tobermory Teuchter: a first-hand
account of life on Mull in the early
years of the 20th century**
Peter Macnab
ISBN 0 946487 41 3 PBK £7.99

The Last Lighthouse
Sharma Kraustopf
ISBN 0 946487 96 0 PBK £7.99

Bare Feet and Tackety Boots
Archie Cameron
ISBN 0 946487 17 0 PBK £7.95

Come Dungeons Dark
John Taylor Caldwell
ISBN 0 946487 19 7 PBK £6.95

MUSIC AND DANCE

Highland Balls & Village Halls
GW Lockhart
ISBN 0 946487 12 X PBK £6.95

**Fiddles & Folk: a celebration of the
re-emergence of Scotland's musi-
cal heritage**
GW Lockhart
ISBN 0 946487 38 3 PBK £7.95

FOOD AND DRINK

Edinburgh & Leith Pub Guide
Stuart McHardy
ISBN 0 946487 80 4 PBK £4.99

SPORT

**Over the Top with the Tartan Army
(Active Service 1992-97)**
Andrew McArthur
ISBN 0 946487 45 6 PBK £7.99

Ski & Snowboard Scotland
Hilary Parke
ISBN 0 946487 35 9 PBK £6.99

**Pilgrims in the Rough: St Andrews
beyond the 19th hole**
Michael Tobert
ISBN 0 946487 74 X PBK £7.99

CARTOONS
Broomie Law
Cinders McLeod
ISBN 0 946487 99 5 PBK £4.00

Luath Press Limited
committed to publishing well written books worth reading

LUATH PRESS takes its name from Robert Burns, whose little collie Luath (*Gael.*, swift or nimble) tripped up Jean Armour at a wedding and gave him the chance to speak to the woman who was to be his wife and the abiding love of his life. Burns called one of *The Twa Dogs* Luath after Cuchullin's hunting dog in *Ossian's Fingal*. Luath Press grew up in the heart of Burns country, and now resides a few steps up the road from Burns' first lodgings in Edinburgh's Royal Mile.

Luath offers you distinctive writing with a hint of unexpected pleasures.

Most UK and US bookshops either carry our books in stock or can order them for you. To order direct from us, please send a £sterling cheque, postal order, international money order or your credit card details (number, address of cardholder and expiry date) to us at the address below. Please add post and packing as follows: UK – £1.00 per delivery address; overseas surface mail – £2.50 per delivery address; overseas airmail – £3.50 for the first book to each delivery address, plus £1.00 for each additional book by airmail to the same address. If your order is a gift, we will happily enclose your card or message at no extra charge.

ILLUSTRATION: IAN KELLAS

Luath Press Limited
543/2 Castlehill
The Royal Mile
Edinburgh EH1 2ND
Scotland
Telephone: 0131 225 4326 (24 hours)
Fax: 0131 225 4324
email: gavin.macdougall@luath.co.uk
Website: www.luath.co.uk